Critical Guides to Spanish Te.

EDITED BY J. E. VAREY AND A. D. .

Critical Guides to Spanish Texts

LOPE DE VEGA

El caballero de Olmedo

J. W. Sage

Senior Lecturer in Spanish at King's College
University of London

Grant & Cutler Ltd *in association with*
Tamesis Books Ltd 1974

© Grant & Cutler Ltd., 1974
ISBN 0 900411 65 1
Printed in England at
The Compton Press Ltd., Salisbury, Wilts.
for
GRANT & CUTLER LTD
11 BUCKINGHAM STREET, LONDON, W.C.2

Contents

References

All references to *El caballero de Olmedo* by Lope de Vega are to the edition by Francisco Rico (2nd edition, Salamanca, 1970). References to the Selected Critical Bibliography on pp. 106-9 are indicated thus: (6, 179-188). References to the text of the play are by lines except where otherwise indicated.

All spellings of old texts have been modernized. All italics are mine unless disowned.

I Introduction

Probably no other play of the Spanish Golden Age has attracted more attention than *El caballero de Olmedo* by Lope Félix de Vega Carpio. Almost everyone who has written about it agrees that it has peculiar fascination. But there agreement ends. Indeed, no Golden Age play has caused more disagreement among commentators of Spanish literature. Clearly, then, from the start we have to face the likelihood that our play is a work – like, say, *Hamlet* or *Don Quixote* – that is too elusive or complex for one man to measure: a play which invites each man to ponder his own response to it.

If, then, Lope's play is of its nature open to different interpretations, I should not like the reader to think that this book sets out to be a guide to *the* interpretation or *the* approach. The posthumous dialogue between Lope and his commentators is far from over. All this book can or should do is to formulate some apt questions, to provide some relevant information so that each reader may respond to them, to outline some of the most illuminating answers that have been given to date (as well as two or three suggestions of my own) – and to expose those answers which seem to commit the literary critic's besetting sin: that of looking only for his own face on the page before him, of offering up an interpretation which reveals more of himself than of the author, of rarefying cerebrally and solemnly in the study what should be experienced commonsensibly in the theatre. Though Lope, from about 1615, began to realize that his drama was also literature to be handed down to posterity, he obviously went on writing plays as plays. In trying to decide whether an interpretation is valid, I shall apply three basic tests: (1) Has the interpreter read the play *as a play* with proper care and respect so that what he says is based upon what we may reasonably suppose Lope expected to be seen and heard in the theatre? (2) Since, all too often, the text can no longer speak for itself, what did Lope and/or other Lopean dramatists say in other relevant contexts? (3) What light do

Lope's sources throw upon his own interpretation of the "Caballero de Olmedo" story? But our final purpose will always be to clarify what Lope intended this text to mean as a play on the stage in his day. After all, what should the final purpose of dramatic criticism be but to elucidate how a play was and should be performed?

The best general study of Lope de Vega's work is, in my view, that by José Fernández Montesinos (27); the breadth of his reading and the depth, sensitivity and commonsense of his criticism may not be immediately apparent, but the more of Lope one reads the more one comes to respect this scholar.

There are, again in my view (and henceforth may this caveat be taken for granted?), only three studies of Lope's *El caballero de Olmedo* which are solid, well-balanced and illuminating. One of these is not now indispensable to the ordinary student: that by the great pioneer of modern Spanish scholarship, don Marcelino Menéndez y Pelayo. His study (5) is still not really outdated and indeed it is still sometimes quietly plundered, but inevitably it has been absorbed and surpassed. The two essential studies are by Francisco Rico (1) in Spanish and Mario Socrate (4) in Italian. My debts to Rico's masterly surveys are as obvious as they are great; the introduction and notes to his edition of our play (1) should be read as an indispensable complement to this guide. Socrate's study is the most thoughtful and stimulating essay available. Neither of these fine scholars will expect us to regard him as above criticism. Even Rico loses his focus sometimes; even Socrate has some wilful moments. (I have summarized Socrate more fully than Rico because most students of our play will not have Italian.) Wardropper is also recommended for his shrewd summary of many critical opinions from Menéndez y Pelayo onwards (6, 179-88) where they help to map out his chosen line of argument, but he has in consequence given short shrift to other views, especially to those of two of the most important scholars: Montesinos, Socrate and in part Rico. Most students will find Wardropper's line of approach stimulating but he will not expect any student to feel under an obligation to follow it. The distinction of being the most provocative writer on our play has been Parker's, partly (see below, p. 66) because he has been misunderstood. My survey of commentaries over the last five years or so suggests that the weight of critical opinion has swung against his approach to this play, but it remains one to be considered by all students. Brief judgments of other studies will be found in the Selected Bibliography, but in general the student might like to note that Trueblood has other studies which are always worth reading, and that for plain commonsense two critics stand out – Marín (7) and Perez (8).

Lope de Vega was Spain's most fertile dramatist. No one knows exactly how many plays he wrote, but certainly over 800 (and a mass of other works): over five times as many as Calderón, perhaps over twenty times as many as Shakespeare. This means that Lope wrote at something like white heat. This in turn has led critics to conclude, often to his detriment in contrast with Calderón, that Lope wrote his plays with gay abandon. Yet one thing which any careful study of *El caballero de Olmedo* must surely put beyond reasonable doubt is that Lope wrote it with meticulous care. Another common assumption is that his plays were based upon stereotyped figures, and rigid ideas fixed for him by the Counter-Reformation. Yet our play is clearly different in certain important respects from the general run of seventeenth-century pot-boilers, not least because it turns upon a kind of character study of don Alonso. Another – again often compared unfavourably with Calderón – is that Lope's plays lack "structure". The student will, I hope, think hard about this favoured word in present-day criticism and ponder the suggestion that our play achieves *as a play* a dramatic coherence as convincing as the more cerebral structures detected by some writers in plays by Calderón. Another assumption is that Lope was pushed into spooning out entertainment for the masses rather than edification for the ignorant or delectation for the élite. A proper answer to this allegation is beyond my scope, but the student will find that Montesinos (27) goes to the heart of the problem. Briefly, though: Do not writers such as Lope or Shakespeare show that mass entertainment, in obliging an artist to grapple with the un-ending problem of how to relate ideals to everyday life, en-courages him to create perspectives and induce tensions which are a powerful source of artistic merit?

2 Date and first performance

The deduction that the play was composed about 1620, with a probable terminal date of 1621, has been generally accepted. (1622 is sometimes given as the terminal date; this is a mistake, following a slip by Montesinos.) The arguments leading to this deduction have been neatly summarized by Rico (*1*, 43 & 74). Socrate (*4*, 96-105) argues that a later date remains possible; he seems to me right only insofar as it remains a mere possibility. A date earlier than 1618 is unlikely. Lope's play was first published in 1641 (*1*, 64-6).

For our present purposes, what matters most about the date of composition is that Lope, *el Fénix de España*, wrote our play when he was nearly sixty. If anyone is tempted to think that this means he was bordering on senility, let him note that masterpieces such as *El castigo sin venganza*, the *Egloga a Claudio*, *La Dorotea* were still to come. And if anyone is tempted to conclude that he was now concerned to write only correct or solemn or spiritual meditations, let him remember that the part-jocular, part-satirical *Rimas . . . de Burguillos*, and the wickedly funny *La gatomaquia* were also still to come. Lope had reached maturity, but this is no reason for supposing that *El caballero de Olmedo* would be more solemn or orthodox or didactic than other plays had been. But we might do well to remind ourselves that it is a play about a young man who is an expressive lover, a knight of a military order, highly honourable and honoured, written by an old man who had been a notorious lover, was a knight of a military order, had been banished for disgraceful behaviour and yet highly honoured. Lope had reason to look with both a sympathetic and a critical eye at don Alonso in our play. Socrate (*4*, 100-22) proposes that at this period Lope's works were marked by a growing sense of disillusion both with his own life and with contemporary Spain, and that he linked this with a growing interest in Spanish history by way of compensation as well as with more artistic awareness. Not everything that Socrate says here is convincing but he does provide further evidence for the view that Lope brought to the play a deep sense of disillusion about the value to the world of the noble-minded hero.

Where was "El caballero de Olmedo" first performed?

Probably in a public theatre (*corral*); wherever it was done, seventeenth-century actors "would have expected to find much the same stage conditions in each *corral* to which they came" (35, 233). We do not know which company of actors gave the first performance, though it is tempting to speculate (see below, p. 20).

A more important question for our purposes is: How was it performed? Some guesswork is involved here but the work of Shergold and Varey[1] gives us a firm basis. Lope probably wrote our play in the expectation that it would be acted on a large wooden stage at one end of a fairly large enclosure, with a narrow roof along the sides plus perhaps a canvas awning as the only coverings. The audience would be large (perhaps running into hundreds in Madrid). Most of them were at a distance from the stage that would encourage the actors – not to say the audience – to shout, yet some, the more privileged and important, would be within whispering distance. A curtain at the back of the stage could be pulled aside to reveal further scenes or a girl's window such as the *reja* of Inés's house in our play, but at this time in the public theatre there was a minimum of stage business. Thanks mainly to Lope himself, the theatre had become the chief source of popular entertainment (on a par with television today). Plays, said the sober J. de Santamaría in 1614 or 1615, were "ya tan ordinarias como la comida". Actors were idolized (and castigated by moralists) under a star-system as pervasive as Hollywood's in its heyday. Conservatives never ceased from decrying the theatre as a cesspit of vice, while "progressives" argued fervently that the artist had the right to dramatize both good and bad "indifferent-ly"[2]. Given, then, the controversial background, the physical dis-

---

[1] N. D. Shergold, *A History of the Spanish Stage from Medieval Times until the End of the Seventeenth Century* (Oxford, 1967); N. D. S. and J. E. Varey, "Some Palace Performances of Seventeenth-century Plays", *Bulletin of Hispanic Studies*, XL (1963), 212-244; etc.

[2] Sage, "Texto y realización de *La estatua de Prometeo* y otros dramas musicales de Calderón", *Hacia Calderón*, ed. H. Flasche (Berlin, 1970), 37-8; cf R. D. F. Pring-Mill, "La 'victoria del hado' en *La vida es sueño*", *ibid.*, 57-60.

position and "dead" acoustics of the *corral*, we may imagine that actors would be inclined to project their parts as larger than life, yet try to please the élite with subtleties of expression. And given the star-system, the concentration upon acting rather than upon stage-effects, and the notorious quickness of the rowdies to hiss or to applaud as the mood took them, hero and heroine could be expected to put themselves across as just that – hero and heroine. Everyone loves a hero. Nevertheless, there would be many in the audience, as we shall see, who would have good cause to feel that heroics had helped to bring Spain low. Wit and *discreteo* (ingenious or refined dialogue) and other stylistic niceties were, on the other hand, much in demand.

If there is one salient point which emerges from this glance at the seventeenth-century public theatre, it is perhaps that conditions were such as to encourage the actor to perform don Alonso in our play as a larger-than-life though not unsubtle hero whose heroics would have seemed of dubious practical value to some in the audience. This is not much more than guesswork, of course, but it is a point worth making because it will emerge again and again from other considerations too. We may object, furthermore, that what the play-producers gave seventeenth-century audiences was not necessarily what Lope intended his plays to give, and there is evidence for this objection[3]. But, on balance, it would seem sensible to conclude that Lope knew his actors and wrote for them plays which were performed generally as he had envisaged.

---

[3]See, for example, Lope's *epístola Al contador Gaspar de Barrionuevo* ("Gaspar, ni imaginéis que con dos cartas . . . "), *Rimas*, ed. G. Diego (Madrid, 1963), 416.

3 *Literary traditions behind the Caballero de Olmedo*

Why did Lope choose to write a play about a knight from Olmedo? One answer often given in general terms is that Lope was an autobiographical artist (*27*, 8, 23, etc.) and that the "nobleman from Olmedo" reflects Lope's own snobbish longing to be regarded as noble. There is very possibly some substance in this allegation, but it is obviously too facile to serve as literary criticism and, anyway, it fails to do justice to the essential Lope. Given space and goodwill, one could demonstrate, largely on the basis of his illuminating *Respuesta . . . al papel que escribio un señor destos reynos a Lope de Vega Carpio en razon de la nueva poesia*[4], his quasi-self-portrait in *La Dorotea*, and his poems, that Lope was a contradictory, meditative and self-critical artist (*27*, 1-17, 65-81, etc.; *7*, *10*, *11*, *41*, *46*). On balance, though, this point could provide another piece of evidence that Lope saw in Alonso a hero, but a hero who was not above criticism.

The specific answer to our question usually given so far is that Lope took as the basis of our play a traditional song which everyone had learned at his mother's knee (*1*, 23-4, 29-30, 43, 50-1). I now have to suggest that this is a simple mistake (as well as an object lesson in how *a priori* theories can blind even the most clear-sighted scholars). The theory is at root one postulated by Pedrell and developed by Menéndez Pidal: that Spanish culture is characterized by a peculiar persistence of its folklore. When Pedrell came across a sixteenth-century song called *El caballero*, he jumped to the conclusion that this was the traditional ballad upon which *El caballero de Olmedo* was based; though he never bothered to note the words of this song, his guess was taken as fact by everyone who followed because it suited the fashionable theory. The details need not concern us here (see *38*), but the simple truth of the matter is that there is no evidence whatsoever for believing that *El caballero de Olmedo* by Lope, or in any of the known versions, is based upon this sixteenth-century song. *El*

[4]*La filomena* (Madrid, 1621), 190.

caballero was indeed a well-known song towards the middle of
the sixteenth century[5]. It was indeed a song with words written
within a well-established European convention, the words as
printed being a refined development of the *serranilla* or perhaps
pastourelle[6] and having nothing to do with the words "Que de
noche le mataron . . ." of the song in our play. There is reason to
suppose that Góngora knew the lyric of the sixteenth-century
Caballero. There is no evidence to connect it with the murder of
Juan de Vivero in 1521 (see below, p. 17), still less to connect it
with any of the accounts or artistic recreations of the "Caballero
de Olmedo" in the seventeenth century. The (very beautiful) tune
of *El caballero* of about 1550 has indeed something of the style of
an old ballad about it (*38*) but there is no reason to suppose
that this tune would have survived into the seventeenth century,
for the popular songs characteristic of the late sixteenth and the
seventeenth centuries were of a new type. So important was the
"newness" of a seventeenth-century song that it would be called
"viejo" if it was more than a decade old (*38*). All we know
about the song in our play (i.e. "Que de noche le mataron . . .")
is that it first appears in print in 1606 in the anonymous play
called *El caballero de Olmedo o la viuda por casar*, licensed for
performance in 1607, and then appears in text after text in various
forms, especially over the next fifteen years (and beyond) (*1*, 29-
37). In short, the song about the "Caballero de Olmedo" was in
vogue early in the seventeenth century. What sort of song was it?
No one has found the music. But there are clues. In the 1606
play, the words are said to have been written by a young "caba-

---

[5]Arrangements of the song were made by: N. Gombert ("Decilde al
,caballero . . . "), *Cancionero de Upsala* [1556], ed. R. Mitjana and J. Bal y Gay
(Mexico City, 1944), 58 and 125; Diego Pisador, *Libro de música de vihuela*
(Salamanca, 1552), f.4 ("Decilde . . . " – "Dejalde . . . " in the *tabla* is an
error); Cristóbal de Morales, *Missa Desilde al cavallero*, *Opera omnia*, VII, ed. H.
Anglés (Barcelona, 1964), 58; Antonio de Cabezón, *Obras de música para tecla,
arpa y vihuela*, III, ed. H. Anglés (Barcelona, 1966), 66 ("Diferencias sobre el
canto [variations on the theme] del Cavallero"); Juan Vásquez, *Recopilacion
de sonetos y villancicos a quatro y a cinco* [1560], ed. H. Anglés (Barcelona,
1946), 47 and 224 ("Por vida de mis ojos / el caballero . . . "). See also M.
Querol Gavaldá, "La canción popular en los organistas españoles del siglo XVI",
Anuario musical, XXI (1966), 69-73.
    [6]A. D. Deyermond, *A Literary History of Spain: the Middle Ages* (London
and New York, 1971), 19.

llero" passing through the village and set to a tune with guitar accompaniment by a servant of his ("un criado suyo músico") (*43*, 158-64). The same tune was presumably used as the basis of the *Baile* (stage-interlude, see p. 20) at about the same time. Alonso in our play (2369-71) describes the music of the song as non-rustic, sweet and refined. In short, the only evidence available to us so far suggests that the song "Que de noche . . ." was looked upon not as a popular song transmitted by any kind of oral tradition but a refined song composed by professionals. (This does not mean that such a refined song could not then enter into oral tradition, but that is another matter . . .) Now, in our play, this song is supposed to have been either composed by or transmitted by Fabia (2383, 2403-6). Let us think twice, then, before we accept the arguments of those critics who link the song and Fabia with the popular soul of Spain . . .

We shall not have to go over all the details of the sources of and references to the "Caballero de Olmedo" story, since Perez and Rico (*8*, 7-11; *9*, 243-50; *1*, 25-45; *3*) have summarized these succinctly for us. Nevertheless, now that I have managed to cut some of the ground from under our feet, we must move more carefully; the reader must be prepared to question a few other commonly held assumptions.

Was the "Caballero de Olmedo" based upon the murder of Juan de Vivero in 1521?

So far it has been taken for granted that it was, or at least that the "Caballero de Olmedo" tradition stemmed from the murder. However, since the supposedly traditional song has always been regarded as evidence for this belief, we must look at the murder more closely. The event is recounted in one sixteenth-century manuscript account and several seventeenth-century versions (*1*, 24-8; *8*, 9-10; *9*, 245-51). It concerns a squalid squabble resulting in the murder of Juan de Vivero by Miguel Ruiz in 1521, i.e. in the reign of the Emperor Charles V. None of the known artistic re-creations of the story places it in this period, nor uses the names Juan de Vivero[7] or Miguel Ruiz, nor refers to the influence of the

---

[7]The lines "sangre tienes de Vibero / con que honras un Jirón", referring to Alonso, were not written by the author in the original MS; see *44*, 169.

mother over her son Miguel, nor to the trivial (outward) cause of
the squabble (9, 246 & 251), nor to the fact that Juan de Vivero
was married, nor to the fact that both *murderer and victim* were
from Olmedo (9, 247). On the other hand, nearly all versions con-
cur with the documented facts of the 1521 affair in locating the
murder between Olmedo and Medina del Campo, in pointing to
an affront to personal honour as a motive (but not jealousy arising from love), in underlining the nobility of Juan de Vivero
(though not his being known as the "Caballero de Olmedo") and
in stigmatizing the deed as ignoble and cold-blooded murder
carried out in an ambush by Ruiz accompanied by servants bearing arms other than swords (9, 247-8). Furthermore, the 1521
affair was a local issue (9; 8, 10), not a national scandal likely to
reach many ears outside Olmedo or Medina. On balance, then,
allowing for the gaps in our knowledge, for artistic licence on the
part of the teller of a tale, for the intrusion of commonplaces such
as jealousy or *pundonor*, and so on, it seems clear that the 1521
murder of Vivero by Ruiz was not the sole source and probably
not the main source of the "Caballero de Olmedo" story.

    Was the main source, then, a traditional song or popular type
of ballad deriving from this murder? If so, no-one has found it
nor any reference to it earlier than the date of the vogue of the
"Caballero de Olmedo" at the beginning of the seventeenth
century. The song in our play ("Que de noche le mataron . . .")
is recorded only by Lope and (in minor variants all bearing a
family likeness) in seventeenth-century plays, poems and chronicled accounts; furthermore, these latter accounts do not have the
force of separate evidence since they derive at least in part from
these plays and poems (1, 23-43; 3). There is a twentieth-century
version by J. R. Jiménez (4, 154) but this too presumably draws
upon the song in Lope's play. Rico (1, 30), however, points to the
following lines in a poem written by Castillejo before 1550 :

> Caballero de Medina
> mal amenazado me han.

The possibility that these words come from some lost ballad about
the "Caballero de Olmedo" dating from the first half of the sixteenth century seems at first sight to be confirmed by Correas (in

his *Vocabulario de refranes*, published 1627), since he repeats precisely these words, adding that they refer "al [caballero] de Olmedo" (*1*, 30). But this is not as certain as Correas thought it was. In the first place, Castillejo's lines name "caballeros de Medina" who have "threatened" some person, whereas the documents relating to the 1521 affair name only one man (Ruiz) among the miscreants who might be considered a "caballero" (although he is not so described), and anyway he is not from Medina but is a "vecino . . . de Olmedo" (9, 247); furthermore, the documents underline not a "threat" to Vivero's life but the way he was murdered in an ambush without warning. (There are, however, other figures – mother, relatives, servant-accomplices – lurking in the background in the documented accounts) (9, 247-51). On the other hand, we do know that these two lines and at least four other lines in Castillejo's pastiche[8] echo the ballad of the *Quejas de doña Lambra*. In default of other evidence, I am driven to the conclusion that the two lines quoted are taken from a ballad related not to the 1521 affair or to the "Caballero de Olmedo" but to some other lyric involving a woman's grievance and some kind of enmity between Medina and (credibly) Olmedo. If this proves correct, then it will provide further evidence that the "Caballero de Olmedo" legend arose from a history of enmity between Medina and Olmedo (see below, p. 91). What, then, could have led Correas to associate these two lines with the "Caballero de Olmedo" story? Since he was writing (1627 or so) in the wake of a spate of plays, songs, dances and poems about the "Caballero de Olmedo" that flooded the first two decades of the seventeenth century, the answer could be that he simply mistook a vogue for a tradition. Nor does the fact that, in his *Arte de la lengua española castellana* of 1625, he gives a version of the song as an example of "old" *seguidillas* (*1*, 29), mean necessarily that it was more than ten or twenty years old, for he shared the seventeenth-century attitude whereby a piece was "old" if it had been known for more than a decade[9].

[8]*Obras,* ed. J. Domínguez Bordona, II (Madrid, 1927), 244-8.
[9]Cf for example: "¿Zarabanda? . . . está muy vieja", Lope, *La villana de Getafe, Obras escogidas,* ed. F. C. Sainz de Robles (Aguilar, Madrid, 1964 etc.), 1463; the sarabande came into vogue towards the end of the sixteenth century, and this play was published in 1621.

In short, neither Castillejo nor Correas offers any substantial evidence that a song about the "Caballero de Olmedo" existed before 1606.

The "Baile del Caballero de Olmedo"

Some confusion exists about this too, so the reader must bear with me still while we scrutinize minutiae. *Baile* was a word used in Spain from the Renascence onwards to mean a popular type of dance as distinct from a *danza* which was of more courtly type[10]. Early in the seventeenth century the *baile* was caught up in the urgent need to season the theatrical fare on the public stage, and so was turned into a short (usually less than 250 lines) play that was part-spoken, part-sung and part-danced. (In this form it was roughly the equivalent of the Italian *intermezzo*, the French *intermède* and the English interlude). Though popular in the sense that it aimed to entertain plebeians, the words of this interlude were more often than not refined. Indeed, such *bailes* were based frequently at this time (that is during most of Lope's lifetime) upon poems by Góngora and by Lope himself[11] as well as upon existing novels and plays[12]. Now, one of the most successful actors in and writers of these interludes about the time Lope wrote *El caballero de Olmedo* (our play) was Alonso de Olmedo[13]. In 1617, in the *Septima parte* of Lope's plays, there was printed a *Vayle famoso del Cavallero de Olmedo compuesto por Lope de Vega* (*1*, 35-7); or the *Baile del Caballero de Olmedo* for short. In this *Baile*, as in Lope's play, the hero is Alonso of Olmedo. Mere coincidence? Is it not much more likely that the actor-producer Alonso de Olmedo wrote the *Baile*; or that the *Baile* was written by someone else for him to perform? By Lope, then? Some

[10]At some stage, the *Baile del Caballero de Olmedo* may have been a *danza*. See J. Castro Escudero, "Bailes y danzas en el teatro de Lope de Vega", *Les Langues Néo-latines*, CLVI (1961), 59.

[11]Rita Goldberg, "Un modo de subsistencia del romancero nuevo: romances de Góngora y de Lope de Vega en bailes del Siglo de Oro", *Bulletin Hispanique*, LXXII (1970), 59 etc.

[12]See *passim*: *Colección de entremeses, loas, bailes, jácaras y mojigangas desde fines del siglo XVI a mediados del XVIII*, ed. E. Cotarelo y Mori, *Nueva Biblioteca de Autores Españoles*, XVII and XVIII (Madrid, 1911).

[13]R. Goldberg, "Un modo de subsistencia", etc., 57-8; N. D. Shergold, *A History of the Spanish Stage* (Oxford, 1967), 291 and 533.

scholars (5; *1*, 36) have felt that the phrase "compuesto por Lope de Vega" did not mean that the *Baile* was written by Lope. Others (see *1*, 36) have taken "compuesto por Lope de Vega" to mean what it appears to mean. The truth is, of course, that we have not enough evidence to be sure; nevertheless, the attribution to Lope is a piece of positive evidence which ought to be respected. The naming of an author ("compuesto por Lope de Vega") in this and other collections of *bailes* was unusual. There must have been some particular reason for doing so here. The most likely reasons are these: that the editor (or publisher) thought Lope wrote the words of the song upon which the *Baile* was based; or that he thought Lope wrote the play upon which the *Baile* would then have been based; or simply that he thought Lope wrote the *Baile del Caballero de Olmedo*.

This means that we ought to keep an open mind about the possibility that, one way or another, Lope de Vega himself was the creator of the song "Que de noche le mataron . . ." in the form that we know it. *El caballero de Olmedo* is one of a number of plays by Lope which in the past have been supposed to be based upon traditional folksongs. Most of these have been shown by now to be based in fact upon lyrics written by Lope himself, though drawing in varying degrees upon traditional song and proverbial matter.[14] Perhaps our play will also be found to show that Lope created popular traditions rather than borrowed them.

*   *   *   *

Now let us try to see if we have cleared a path for ourselves. (1) The song "Que de noche le mataron . . ." (with minimal variants) was certainly in vogue early in the seventeenth century but there is no evidence that it was a traditional song going back to the sixteenth century.

[14]See for example: Jerome Aaron Moore, *The 'Romancero' in the Chronicle-legend Plays of Lope de Vega* (Philadelphia, 1940), 146-9 etc.; M. Frenk Alatorre, "Un desconocido cantar de los comendadores: fuente de Lope", *Homenaje a William L. Fichter* (see *12*), 211-222; J. B. Avalle-Arce, "Pedro Carbonero y Lope de Vega: tradición y comedia", *ibid.*, 59-70; F. López Estrada, "La canción 'Al val de Fuente Ovejuna' de la comedia *Fuenteovejuna* de Lope", *ibid.*, 453-68; María Cruz García de Enterría, "Función de la 'letra para cantar' en las comedias de Lope de Vega; comedia engendrada por una canción", *Boletín de la Biblioteca Menéndez y Pelayo*, XLI (1965), 3-62, etc.

(2) Its first appearance in print was in 1606 in the anonymous *Caballero de Olmedo* play; it may not have existed as a popular song until this play helped to popularize it.

(3) The evidence suggests that it was a refined song rather than a folksong, though it became "popular" in the sense of well known.

(4) It served as the basis of the *Baile del Caballero de Olmedo* published in 1617. Since songs by Lope (and Góngora) were often made into *bailes* (interludes) at this time, the song therefore probably preceded the *Baile*; since the song is in the 1606 play, the play therefore probably preceded the *Baile*.

(5) The *Baile*, or the song or the play upon which it would have been based, was published as "composed by Lope de Vega"; the available evidence suggests that this *Baile* was written by Lope, or at least that the words of the song were his; we cannot rule out the possibility that Lope had a hand in writing the 1606 play.

The Anonymous Play "El caballero de Olmedo o la viuda por casar" of 1606

No-one seems to have had a kind word for this melodrama. Generally it has been found not good enough to be Lope's (*1*, 38-40); we might object, though, that Lope did write some bad plays. Menéndez y Pelayo proposed that the author was Claramonte, but this was just one of his majestic guesses; Juliá Martínez argued for Cristóbal de Morales (see *1*, 40, note) but this too amounts to little more than a guess. Don Marcelino also hinted at the possibility of a third play about "El caballero de Olmedo" now lost (*5*, 87); though Rico does so too, so far this remains another guess (*1*, 44, note).

Don Marcelino went even further : he concluded that Lope knew nothing about this 1606 play. Rico and Blecua (*1*, 44; *14*, 24) tend to the same conclusion but most commentators have taken the opposite view (*27*, 23; *8*, 13; *4*, 150-1; *7*, 4; *15*, 344; *36*). This is another matter which the serious student must decide for himself; my view is that Lope not only knew the 1606 play but took it as raw material for his play of about 1620. Indeed, there are other reasons for coming to this tentative conclusion in addition to those suggested by these scholars. In both plays the given name of the hero is Alonso (as it is in most of the artistic re-creations of the story) whereas it is Juan in the 1521 affair. In both plays there is textual emphasis upon the hero as a greatly admired, noble, valorous Castilian champion in whom filial duty even supersedes passion. In both, the murderer's claim to the hand of the heroine is backed by royal patronage (as noted by *8*, 14). In both, jealousy and envy turn an amorous rival into a cold-blooded villain. In both there is a notable disparity between initial comedy and final tragedy. In both, the song is crucial. Since there is no evidence that a traditional song existed that might have explained these common factors, we are driven to the provisional conclusion that the later play imitated the former.

In interpreting our play, then, I shall take the argument that Lope re-wrote the 1606 play as a credible one, and use a comparison between the two plays as one of my criteria.

Faced with this uncertainty about Lope's sources, where should we turn for enlightenment? It seems to me that there are three other issues which must have been very much in Lope's mind when he began to compose our play; the reader should be warned, however, that they are my own views which have yet to be subjected to the test of scrutiny by other critics. These issues concern the significance of the "caballero" in literature and in life, and the relevance of events in the reign of Juan II of Castile. Let us first look more closely at the "caballero".

4 The figure of the knight in Lope's day

(a) In Literature

A full answer to this question is well beyond my scope; I shall select only a few points relevant to our play.

I shall take "caballero" here to mean a nobleman who has been, or at least could be supposed to have been, raised to honourable military rank by the king; equivalent to "knight" in this sense.

The "caballero" had long been a topic of Spanish poetry. In the middle of the sixteenth century he is still there, much as he had been before, in *villancicos*, *romances* and *serranillas*, as a young nobleman admired and desired in the main even when the poem has been written from the point of view of a girl seduced by him. But one of the changes that has come about concerns the tendency to give now to a "caballero" the amorous, mischievous rôle previously given generally to an "escudero". "La sustitución de la palabra *caballero* en vez de *escudero* en los romances y cantares tradicionales ocurre después de 1519 [?], y está consumada antes de 1550; ocurre pues exactamente en tiempos de Carlos V, que es cuando la nobleza acaba de perder su carácter militar para convertirse en cortesano . . . El *caballero* sustituto no representa, como el antiguo *escudero*, un joven adolescente . . ."[15] Here then is a relatively new type of "caballero": young but now fully-fledged, amorous, admired for his courtly polish rather than his military bravura. Now, this was the literary "caballero" Lope (born 1562) would have cut his poetic teeth on. There is literary precedent for the courtly-chivalrous language of don Alonso in our play; there is more remote precedent for his military arts. As Lope matured artistically, he could not have failed to note, however, that a more critical or quizzical attitude towards the "caballero" in poetry of traditional type was beginning to make itself felt towards the turn of the century. The following lyrics have

[15]R. Menéndez Pidal, *De primitiva lírica española y antigua épica* (Buenos Aires, 1951), 137-9.

n only because they are of more obvious relevance to
even so, they will serve to mark out the main path of
nt.

th century and later :

> Aquel caballero, madre,
> que de amores me habló,
> más que a mí le quiero yo . . .
>> *Cancionero musical de palacio,* ed. H.
>> Anglés, no. 329; etc., etc.

at 1530-1550 :

> *El caballero*
> Decilde al caballero
> que non se quexe,
> que yo le doy mi fe
> que non le dexe.
> Decilde al caballero
> que non se quexe
> en ascondido,
> que yo le doy mi fe
> que non le dexe . . .
>
> Por vida de mis ojos,
> el caballero,
> por vida de mis ojos
> bien os quiero . . .
>> Gombert, Pisador, Morales, Cabezón;
>> Vásquez.

Before 1550 :

> Caballeros de Medina
> mal amenazado me han . . .
>> Quoted by Castillejo.

1610 :

> "Tiempo es, el caballero,
> tiempo es de andar de aquí,
> que tengo la madre brava
> y el veros será mi fin."
> El, contento, fía su robo

de las ancas de un rocín,
y ella, amante, ya su fuga
del caballero gentil.
Decilde a su madre, Amor,
si la viene a buscar,
que una abeja la lleva la flor
a otro mejor colmenar;
picar, picar,
que cerquita está el lugar.
Decilde que no se aflija
y perdone al llanto tierno,
pues granjeó galán yerno
cuando perdió bella hija.

       Góngora, "Apeóse el caballero . . ."

(5) 1597 :

Madre, *el caballero*
que a las *fiestas* sale
a matar los *toros*
sin que ellos le maten . . .
[He has wooed, seduced and abandoned her]
Cuando entre en los *toros*
mañana en la tarde,
mal fuego le queme
todos sus plumajes.
No saque *el valor*,
ni *la lanza* saque
con que antaño hizo
tan *vistosos lances*.
Y al correr la plaza
con *otros galanes*,
caída dé él solo . . .

    Anon., *Las series valencianas del romancero nuevo*,
      ed. A. Rodríguez-Moñino, no. 204.

(6) About 1600 :

No paséis, el caballero,
tantas veces por aquí,
si no, bajaré mis ojos,
juraré que nunca os vi . . .

      Cancionero musical de Turín, no. 31.

The first and second are uncritical expressions of a girl's love for a knight. (The second is the lyric of the song mistakenly supposed to be the basis of our play.) Taking its context into account, the third implies a lack of *caballerosidad* in some "caballeros". The words of the fourth in italics suggest that Góngora is reminiscing piquantly about the "caballero" of the second. The fifth is written from the bitterly critical point of view of a girl ill-used by a knight; the words in italics suggest that there are enough points of contact between this poem and the two *Caballero de Olmedo* plays for the dramatist(s) to have had it in mind. The sixth will serve to show how the girl becomes critical of the nobleman not usually because he courts her but because he does not court her with enough secrecy.

This relatively new attitude towards *caballerosidad* is of course one which soon develops at the turn of the century into deliberate and insistent mockery, sometimes jocular burlesque but more often bitter satire, sometimes of an "hidalgo" but more often specifically of the "caballero". Examples are almost too well-known to need repeating : Leucino in Cueva's *El infamador*; Don Quixote; Quevedo's satires of "caballeros" in poems such as "Poderoso caballero es don Dinero" (a proverbial phrase of the day) or social comment such as *El caballero de la tenaza* or even in the outwardly noble but really mean and hypocritical figure of don Diego in *El buscón*; don Juan of Tirso's *Burlador de Sevilla*; both don Mendo and the Captain in Calderón's *El alcalde de Zalamea*; the spineless "heroes" in Moreto's *El desdén con el desdén* and other comedies; and so on. In literature, at least, there was, then, at the time of the vogue of the "Caballero de Olmedo" story (*c*1606-*c*1620), a well-defined tendency to look askance at "caballeros" and "hidalgos" whether they were of ancient stock ("notoriamente noble") or not.

Was the "hidalgo antiguo" too old an ideal, then, for seventeenth-century literature? Not by any means for everyone. Cervantes gave credible accounts of "caballeros" of long-standing nobility in the heroes of *La gitanilla*, *La española inglesa* and (if his) *La señora Cornelia*. Books of chivalry were no longer staple diet but the Cid ballads were the most widely published of all the old ballads throughout the seventeenth century. Moreto offers

an apparently serious portrayal of genuine *caballerosidad* in his
play *El caballero*. The qualities that this "caballero" displays are
the following.

Military arts:

> la milicia es quien da el grado
> a un perfecto caballero.

Noble blood:

> es un grande caballero
> y eso le debe a su sangre.

Valour, even to the extent of proudly refusing to withdraw or
hide in the face of danger. Generosity, even to the degree of being
magnanimous to his enemies. Rectitude, in that he refuses to
deceive others where he thinks his good name is involved, but not
to the degree of being unwilling to deceive his father in the name
of love – this he readily does because he is "discreto". And of
course he is dashing ("muy galán y muy bizarro"). Let us note in
particular the fact that this model nobleman is prepared to deceive
his elders in the interests of love, since it will serve as a piece of
evidence against the allegation that Alonso is guilty of moral
error in deceiving the father of Inés. In general, these qualities
are so obviously similar to those that characterize don Alonso in
our play, that it comes as no surprise to find Moreto himself
drawing the parallel:

> ¿Si se bautizó en Olmedo?[16]

Don Alonso has become, for Moreto at least, a prototype of the
true knight.

In sum, then, the literary "caballero" of the seventeenth century
was a figure at times still admired for precisely those features
which at other times made him a source of mockery. The "caballero" in seventeenth-century literature seems to have reached a
cross-roads.

When we turn to Lope's plays, we find that they too point in

[16]*Parte diez y nueve de varios* (Madrid, 1662), 289; 293-4, 297, 305; 300; 293;
291; 303; quotation from 294; *Biblioteca de Autores Españoles*, XXXIX, 289, etc.

this respect in two directions. On the one hand there is the true nobleman. In the *auto, El Caballero del Sacramento* (1610), the "caballero" is Christ Himself. The image was a common one, as it was for St. James the patron saint of Spain.[17] This gives a touch of strength to the argument favoured by some critics that Alonso is a Christ-figure. In general "el tema verdaderamente obsesivo en los autos de Lope es el tan candente y vidrioso de la hidalguía, correspondencia bien transparente de una insoslayable realidad social, hidalguía que señala, precisamente, la existencia de honor *a nativitate* . . ." *49*, 100[18]. The belief that "nobility will out" is – almost needless to say – found in secular plays by Lope too (*39*) such as *El caballero de Illescas*. On the other hand, there is the figure who questions or gives cause to question the belief in inherited nobility as well as in recently acquired nobility. In *La dama boba*, Duardo, Liseo and Laurencio are anything but the "caballeros" cast in ideal Neoplatonic mould they purport to be. In *El caballero del milagro*, Luzmán fools aristocratic circles for many years by posing as a nobleman who displays the qualities these aristocrats expected a nobleman to display: lavish style, honourable attitude, valour, poise, refinement and a suave Neoplatonic vocabulary. The unspoken answer to Celia's question in *Santiago el verde* –

> ¿Es mucho hacer caballero
> a un hombre que no lo hace?[19]

is obviously a worldlywise "No, it doesn't take much money or trickery nowadays for a man to be accepted as a *caballero*". Leonardo in *El cuerdo en su casa* is a pretentious "hidalgo de aldea" who is exposed in the end as a pathetic fool. Many other works by Lope are ambivalent, though. Such is *Guzmán el bravo*, a mischievous but subtle novel in the way it plays with the notion of heroic nobility. Or the two plays about *Los Tellos de Meneses*, in more serious vein. And many more (see *39*).

---

[17]See for example: "y encima de su celada/puso una imagen pequeña/del santo Patrón de España/en forma de caballero", Lope, *Valor, fortuna y lealtad, Obras escogidas*, I, ed. Sainz, 463b.

[18] But cf 102, and see below, 33.

[19]*Obras escogidas*, ed. Sainz, 1241a.

In which direction, then, did Lope intend don Alonso of our
play to point? Many commentators, among them those most
worthy of general respect, have felt that Lope intended him to
represent true nobility, a "caballero" as he should be. However,
an increasing number of critics have begun to move so far in the
opposite direction that we would be well advised to make more
sure of our ground before proceeding.

"Quizás la mejor comedia burlesca o de disparates de nuestro
antiguo teatro" for Menéndez y Pelayo (and cf *1*, 60-1) was
Monteser's burlesque of the "Caballero de Olmedo": *El cavallero de Olmedo, fiesta burlesca que se representó a su Magestad,
año 1651.* (There is no record of an earlier performance.) Such
burlesque performances for the court's delectation were common
from about the 1620s; we should be mistaken if we assumed that
they were all just frivolous jokes; the court was, throughout the
seventeenth century, not just a haven for fops and drones but also
an invigorating cultural centre to which many writers from
Cervantes to Calderón aspired. There is, then, justification for
taking a serious look at Monteser's burlesque. Don Marcelino
could not bring himself to believe that Monteser would dare to
burlesque the *Caballero de Olmedo* of Lope himself (5, 87; *1*,
44, note), but the student can make up his own mind about this.
The death scene is characteristic. Rodrigo cheerfully reveals to
Alonso his murderous plan –

ALONSO	Perdonad, no lo sabía.
RODRIGO	¿Venís?
ALONSO	Sí.
RODRIGO	Pues allá espero. (*Vase*)

   . . . .

ALONSO	Pues si el romance lo dice,
	yo ¿qué puedo hacer en esto? (*53*, 169-70).

My impression of this scene (which must of course be taken in
the context of the whole of this rewarding play) is that it is burlesque with a satiric (i.e. seriously critical) edge, that Alonso is
laughable precisely because of his *caballerosidad*, his nobleminded-
ness so ludicrously inappropriate when faced with a man about to
murder him.

Could we not say the same of Lope's don Alonso? Are the seeds of burlesque not in Lope's tragicomedy itself? Monteser was not the only writer to mock our play in the seventeenth century; there are other versions that are more farcical. Yet even in these, there is a comparable note of deliberate ridicule of Alonso's antique, chivalrous pose. So, for example, Villaviciosa in his *Entremés de los sones* (published 1661): "Sale el Caballero con vestido antiguo, ridículo . . ." Or Cañizares in his *Mojiganga de los sones*: "Sale el Caballero vestido de toreador ridículo."[20] Monteser, at any rate, seems to me to be making, humorously, exactly the same point as Saavedra Faxardo (and many other writers of the seventeenth century) made in his *Idea de un príncipe político christiano*, when he wrote: "Sustituye, pues, el ardid a la fuerza . . . La espada en pocas partes puede obrar; la negociación en todas como los árboles se comunican y unen por las raíces".[21] Lope's don Alonso believes in the fellowship of nobility, valour and the sword; with only a touch of the Machiavellian cunning (*discreción*) the seventeenth century held in some regard, he could have averted the tragedy. But then would he have retained the reputation for being honourable which the seventeenth century also held in high regard? This ambivalence is pointedly illustrated in two poems in a collection of song-lyrics put together about the time Lope wrote our play. One expresses admiration for our "Caballero":

> El caballero de Olmedo
> bizarro sale a unas fiestas . . .

The other satirizes an "hidalgo de aldea" (the pretentious village upstart):

> Un hidalgo de una aldea,
> bien hidalgo y mal vestido . . .[22]

[20]*Colección de entremeses* etc., ed. Cotarelo, XVII, ccxxxv-vi.

[21](Antwerp, 1655), 668-9 ("Plura Consilio, Quam Vi").

[22]Hispanic Society of America (New York), MS XVI, *Catálogo de los manuscritos poéticos castellanos* . . . , ed. A. Rodríguez-Moñino and María Brey Mariño (New York, 1965-6), I, 125, 128. In part at least this is a collection of the lyrics of songs of the early seventeenth century.

They are both "noblemen"; the difference between the true and the false is seen in their manner, their dress. This will serve as a piece of evidence against those critics who feel that don Alonso in our play should be seen as foppish and false . . .

Correas, writing about 1625, cites a proverb :

> Yo, ¿qué le debo al caballero?
> Nada no le debo.[23]

How many lips, other than those of disappointed girls within literary traditions, formed that same question and gave that same answer but within the context of imperial decadence? The time has come to think about my second suggestion.

(b) In Everyday Life

The concept of honour in seventeenth-century Spain has been seen in recent years more as a literary convention than a fact of life[24]. Some students might like to leave the matter there. Others might like to consider the rather different argument that follows. (See also 39.)

What evidence is there that nobility in general and *caballerosidad* in particular formed a topic that was debated in real life? Historians provide us with a clear answer : it was a burning topic of Lope's day. The admirable historian Domínguez Ortiz, for one, offers solid bases for concluding that high-ranking Spanish families found it increasingly necessary to wrestle with the minority but growing belief that a man was noble not by right of birth nor even of virtuous behaviour but in consequence of the actual status he had by his own efforts achieved (34, 17, 42, 47, 171-189, 203, 225, 252, 267, 273, 286-319). Ortiz himself suggests that this struggle shows itself in the Lopean theatre in a "mezcla de jerarquía y sana democracia" (34, 17). He and others (cf 39, 25) have pointed to the growing number of middle-class and

---

[23]*Arte de la lengua española* [o] *castellana,* ed. E. Alarcos García (Madrid, 1954), 467.

[24]See for example: C. A. Jones, *"Honor* in Spanish Golden-Age Drama: Its Relation to Real Life and to Morals", *Bulletin of Hispanic Studies,* XXXV (1950), 199-210. Cf J. G. Peristiany, ed. *Honour and Shame: The Values of Mediterranean Society* (London, 1965).

plebeian upstarts, of "nouveaux riches" who laid claim to *de facto* nobility (*34*, 30-47 etc., 180-90, 225, 252, 288). We need hardly add that the majority went on maintaining that true nobility was the unchanging and unchangeable quality the privileged had always taken it to be, something inherited not acquired, something akin to military valour (*34*, 184, 272-3). Yet it is clear that the privileged were beginning to feel shaken by rebellious rumblings from below (*34*, 267-70). I shall try to use the documentation provided by historians in order to make a short list of points which bear upon our play. (All page references are to *34*.)

(1) In the seventeenth century, chivalrous nobility was still greatly admired in theory though looked upon as distinctly antique compared to the increasingly middle-class realities of everyday life (286-7, etc.).

(2) Many who enjoyed the title of "caballero" found themselves being pulled down towards the middle class; "puede advertirse claramente la cesura entre nobles y grandes . . . y los caballeros e hidalgos, destinados a fundirse con las clases medias, cuando no a ser proletarizados" (190-1).

(3) Plebeians who sought to climb up the social scale wanted honour or social "style" rather than wealth as an end in itself, but realized that wealth was a necessary means to social recognition (180-1).

(4) The best proof of nobility in practice was reputation rather than lineage (173-4, 179).

(5) Military deeds could still serve as proof of nobility in the seventeenth century but after 1588 or thereabouts (with the defeat of the Armada) more and more nobles came to show their disenchantment with the belief that honour accrued from military arts (273, etc.).

(6) "Nadie tomó en serio la nobleza de la virtud o de las letras" (311); yet "esta mezcla de rasgos auténticos y bastardos, heroicos y grotescos, es muy propia de una época de transición entre formas de vida, ideales antiguos y otros que aún estaban lejos de concretarse en un sistema coherente" (287).

I concluded from our survey of the "caballero" in literature, that in the seventeenth century he seemed to have reached a crossroads. Our survey of the "caballero" from the historian's angle has brought us to the same point. What makes a man a noble man? The answer was no longer one which could be taken for granted. We seem to have some weighty evidence that our play about the "Nobleman from Olmedo" is a case of art reflecting life.

But there is an obvious yet fundamental objection to this view that *El caballero de Olmedo* reflects a topic of Lope's day: the play is set not in Lope's day but in the fifteenth century during the reign of Juan II of Castile. This brings me to my third suggestion: that the drama repays a scrutiny of its historical background.

Commentators have found some common ground in this area
There are in the play at least two clearly historical figures: Juan
II of Castile (1406-54) and his favourite, the Condestable don
Alvaro de Luna. Nevertheless, the conclusion generally drawn
or implied is that, though the play is traditional, it is not historical
(*5*; *37*; *41*; *1*, 45) because it appears to follow no particular
chronicle and no clear sequence of historical events, and does not
make a central issue of the king and his notorious favourite.
This seems reasonable enough, and some students may feel
inclined to leave the matter there. Yet even here Lope has
managed to provoke a certain measure of disagreement among
his critics, a measure which in my view (see Appendix) ought to
be a little larger.

Menéndez y Pelayo (5, 178) praised Lope's instinct for select-
ing an historical ethos appropriate to his plays. Regarding our
play, he suggested that Lope, by setting it in the reign of Juan II
of Castile, contrived to relate the witchcraft in the drama to the
superstition and sorcery which, he alleges, characterized Juan's
reign (5, 81). The point seems a little forced, though the evidence
cited by don Marcelino has been reinforced by recent studies. We
probably ought to look for other reasons for the dramatist's choice
of period. Nevertheless, Sarrailh (*37*), who has done most work
in this poorly explored area, and others, repeat Menéndez y
Pelayo's conclusion. In general, though, Sarrailh tends to take the
view that Lope made a poor job of adapting his historical background: although his portraits of the weak but poetry-loving
king and the subtle and dominating Condestable are convincing,
his anachronistic and haphazard references to other historical
matters are not (*37*, 337-52; and see *1*, 45, note). Rico adds
authoritative weight to this view, concluding that the historical
matters inserted by Lope into this play are stereotyped and un-
important and that really "todo . . . es de los días de Lope" (*1*,
45). Many students of the play will feel inclined to leave the

matter there : the historical allusions add a few touches of well-
worn colour and little else. However, I suspect that this historical-
political field (not just in our play but in the Lopean theatre
generally) is one which has yet to be properly worked, and that
when it has been we shall see that Lope had a deeper sense of
historical truth than most of his critics. (Some new lines of
approach are suggested in the Appendix.) But at least we ought
to consider seriously the possibility that don Alonso was intended
to be seen as a knight whose style and actions were appropriate
to the times of Juan II of Castile. Perhaps also we may all agree
upon one basic premise : Lope did not intend this drama to be
taken as the kind of historical work where the dramatist was
under any obligation whatsoever to follow the precise chronology
or transcribe literally data taken from his chosen period; anach-
ronisms in a work of art simply do not matter unless they
strain credibility or artistic integrity. If this premise is granted,
there is, from a literary point of view, no reason to spend much
time reciting the list of "errors" of historical fact Lope has been
accused of making in this play. Any student who is interested
will find them best summarized by Sarrailh (37; but see also
Appendix). Our main concern ought to be to decide whether
Lope injected into the drama something of the character of the
reign of Juan II as a meaningful factor. I think he did, but since
this is a fresh point of view which has yet to be properly tested
by other scholars, I have merely outlined the evidence in the
Appendix and shall do no more than touch on a few points here.

Perhaps the root cause of the general allegation that Lope's
handling of history in *El caballero de Olmedo* was weak, lies in
the assumption that the tap-root of the story was the 1521 murder
of Juan de Vivero, and that 1521 was therefore the right period.
But this assumption is open to doubt, as we have seen. Hence,
most critics have implied rather than said that Lope, in locating
his play in the reign of Juan II, chose the wrong period. My suggestion (see Appendix) is that this reign may yet prove to be the
right period in the sense that events leading to the Battle of
Olmedo in 1445 sowed the seeds of the "Caballero de Olmedo"
legend. Anyway, let us assume for the moment that Lope did

know what he was doing, that he did have good reasons for choosing this period. One obvious question arises.

Is the Hero in the Play linked with any Hero of the Time of Juan II of Castile?

The name of the hero in the play is don Alonso Manrique. When Cervantes wanted to underline Quixote's ludicrous notion (Part I, xiii) that Dulcinea came from a family that was as old as the oldest lineages of Castile, he made the "Caballero de la triste figura" name these lineages as the "Cerdas, Manriques, Mendozas y Guzmanes de Castilla". The Manrique clan was indeed regarded as one of the half-dozen most illustrious families in Castile. Who, then, was the head of the illustrious Manrique clan during the reign of Juan II of Castile? From the 1440s at least, he was the Maestre don Rodrigo Manrique de Lara, Conde de Lara (1406-76). Did Lope have Rodrigo Manrique specifically in mind? The evidence suggests that he did, for the qualities ascribed to don Rodrigo Manrique by fifteenth-century accounts are curiously akin to those that characterize don Alonso Manrique in our play. Some of these are set out in the Appendix. Here we need only note that the strongest link of all is valour. Rodrigo Manrique enjoyed a singular reputation as "el más señalado caballero de estos reinos"[25] because of his uncompromising belief in valour; Alonso Manrique is "el más noble, el más valiente,/el más galán caballero/que ciñó espada en Castilla" (2497-9).

Now, despite the evidence to the contrary, let us suppose that Lope knew that a man called Juan de Vivero was murdered in 1521, nearly a century after the date implied in the play for the murder of don Alonso. If Lope did have Juan de Vivero in mind, he made no reference of any kind to him. Fidel Fita, who has done most work on documents referring to the Vivero clan in the sixteenth century, thought nevertheless that Lope's hero was modelled upon Juan de Vivero and that his name, Alonso Manrique, could be explained simply as a piece of poetic licence.[26]

[25]Quoted by R. B. Tate (ed.), Fernando del Pulgar, *Libro de los claros varones de Castilla* (Oxford, 1971), 95-6.
[26]Fidel Fita, "El caballero de Olmedo y la orden de Santiago", *Boletín de la Real Academia de la Historia*, XLVI (1905), 398-422; cf 343-6, 452-74.

This is not very convincing. Much more likely is a link in Lope's mind with Alonso Pérez de Vivero, who was indeed a figure of note during the reign of Juan II, the period of Lope's play. He appears frequently in the chronicles[27] as a privy counsellor, a loyal messenger, Maestre de Calatrava from 1443, and as the victim of murder in 1453 allegedly planned by the Condestable. There are other more tenuous links between the Alonso Pérez of the chronicles and Alonso Manrique in our play (*1*, 44, note), but, on the evidence of the chronicles, the only strong link is murder. We might perhaps argue that Lope had another Alonso Pérez in mind: "don Alfonso [o Alonso] Pérez de Guzmán, principio de la casa de Medina-Sidonia", a clan whose members Lope praises for their "valor"[28]. The emphasis upon valour suggests that this illustrious figure should not be lightly dismissed as a further link, but we are now reaching a stage where explanations are becoming mere guesses.

In sum, there is reason to suppose that Lope modelled the hero of his play upon two notable figures of the period of the play (roughly 1440); there is no textual evidence that he modelled him upon Juan de Vivero, murdered in 1521. Of the two figures of the reign of Juan II, Rodrigo Manrique, with his almost obsessive belief in valour, sheds more light upon the character of don Alonso than does Alonso Pérez de Vivero.

I am not suggesting that the chronicles were Lope's main source for this play; his sources were undoubtedly manifold, and some if not most of these would have been literary rather than historical; we have already glanced at the effect the literary "caballero" must have had upon Lope's artistic sensibility. He might also have had somewhere in his mind, or on his desk, a ballad such as the following (the exact relevance of which is made clearer by events described in the Appendix):

[27]Lorenzo Galíndez de Carvajal, *Crónica del rey don Juan el segundo* etc., *Biblioteca de Autores Españoles*, LXVIII, 553, 554, 559, 586, 608, 611, 612, 613, etc. León de Corral, *Don Alvaro de Luna según testimonios inéditos de la época* (Valladolid, 1915), 69-76. *Crónica del halconero de Juan II, Pedro Carrillo de Huete* [and] *Refundición del halconero por el obispo Don Lope Barrientos*, ed. Juan de Mata Carriazo (Madrid, 1946), 340-3, 374, 410, 417, 437, 443, 471-2, etc.
[28]Lope, *La Arcadia, Obras completas*, I, ed. J. de Entrambasaguas (Madrid, 1965), 71.

> Yo me soy el Infante Enrique
> de Aragón y de Secilia,
> hijo del rey don Fernando,
> nieto del rey de Castilla,
> maestre de Santiago
> de la gran caballería,
> el gran conde de Alburquerque,
> señor de Huete y Gandía,
> señor de muchos vasallos
> en Aragón y Castilla,
> el mayor duque ni conde
> que en España se sabía . . .
> Fortuna . . .
> revolvióme con mi primo
> el rey don Juan de Castilla . . .
> mas don Alvaro de Luna . . .
> hubo de mí grande envidia . . .
> vime señor de Toledo,
> señor del Andalucía . . .
> Hubimos la gran batalla
> cerca de Olmedo esa villa,
> do fuimos todos vencidos
> por muy gran desdicha mía.[29]

More probably still, Lope had in mind the ballads about Juan II's favourite, don Alvaro de Luna; they were so popular in Lope's day that the only likely reason for not having them in mind when composing a play involving don Alvaro would be that familiarity had bred contempt. Indeed, Lope does speak of them as an "enfadoso sujeto", in his play *La prueba de los amigos*[30], written some sixteen years (1604) before he wrote *El caballero de Olmedo*; but at the same time he concedes that they contain "letras que toquen historia". These words reflect his, and his age's, growing awareness of the problem of distinguishing factual history from fiction, tradition and legend – a problem which goes to the root of all of our difficulties in tracing his sources. If there was one quality in these ballads which would

---

[29]Juan Alcina Franch, ed. *Romancero antiguo: I, romances heroicos* (Barcelona, 1969), 212-6.
[30]*Obras escogidas*, ed. Sainz, 1432a.

have impressed him as relevant to the reign of Juan II, it would
have been an overwhelming mood of fateful tragedy. (He might
also have derived from them the idea of Alonso's confrontation
with himself[31].)

[31]See A. Pérez Gómez (ed.), *Romancero de Don Alvaro de Luna (1540-1800)*, (Valencia, 1953), 151 (romance 34), etc.

6 "El caballero de Olmedo" and "La Celestina"

No one has disputed the fact that Lope's play does set out deliberately to recall *La Celestina* (*1*, 54-5). But commentators are in radical disagreement about Lope's reasons for doing so. However, this is one of those matters about which the student can make up his own mind by reading both works carefully. After all, *La Celestina* is a masterpiece and Lope's *El caballero de Olmedo* is not far off it.

La Celestina was first published anonymously in 1499 as *Comedia de Calisto y Melibea*. An expanded version, ascribed to Fernando de Rojas, was published soon afterwards as *Tragicomedia de Calixto y Melibea* and thereafter simply as *La Celestina*. The story tells of how Calixto falls deeply in love with Melibea, uses a wily old sorceress and go-between, Celestina, in order to meet Melibea and make love to her, and later falls accidentally to his death.[32] The book inspired numerous imitations through the sixteenth and seventeenth centuries (cf *1*, 55, note), but the only imitations of comparable quality are by Lope de Vega: our play and *La Dorotea* (though some with good reason would include Delicado's *La lozana andaluza* as well). Both Lope's works could be seen as following *La Celestina* in taking an exceptional interest in character study, though some critics, finding character study irrelevant to the Spanish seventeenth-century stage, have seen the common link as moral error on the part of the lovers. Lope also wrote other less impressive imitations of *La Celestina* (*12*, 373-4; *17*, 53-5; *51*). In general they have a common attitude towards sorcery[33]; where the Celestinesque go-between uses her magic powers to make a girl fall in love *against her will*, the plot ends at least on a note of reprobation. Here, then, is some rather uncertain support for those

[32]See Deyermond, *A Literary History*, 166-170.

[33]Cf Dorotea's words in *La Dorotea*: "Gerarda, si es por mal camino, Dios me libre de que tal intente. Fuera de que yo no sé qué mujer de juicio se vale de hechicerías; que es afrenta grande que lo que no pudieron los méritos lo puedan las violencias", ed. J. M. Blecua (Madrid, 1955), 568 (V. vi).

critics (see below, p. 67) who argue that Lope linked our play
with *La Celestina* because both works present the death of the
lover as poetic justice for the breaking of moral laws. The important question to decide here is how far, if at all, Fabia makes
Inés in our play fall passionately in love by means of sorcery. We
should also remember that the causes of death differ radically. In
La Celestina Calixto dies more or less accidentally (by chance?);
in our play, Alonso is cold-bloodedly murdered (a relatively
innocent victim of malice?).

Montesinos (27) suggested that one reason why Lope imitated *La Celestina* was that it stood for him as an important
model of tragicomedy. Insofar as the Rojas version was published
as a *tragicomedia*, and insofar as both works are mixtures of the
comic and the serious and of figures of high and low status (not
to say figures of high status with both high and lowly qualities),
there is clearly something in this argument. So there is too in the
argument that, since *La Celestina* ends with the tragic death of
the lovers, and Lope constantly refers to the Celestina story
throughout his play, he thereby increased his audience's apprehen-
sion of tragic inevitability. But ought we not to question the
assumption that *La Celestina* would prompt most of the audience
to think of tragic death rather than the pulse of life beating in
the wicked old bawd herself who gave the book its title?

Those who see don Alonso as a kind of parody of the courtly
hero might find some support for their notion in the fact that
Calixto is in part such a parody.[34]

The disagreement centres upon the function of magic in our
play. Critics are divided between those who find Fabia deployed
seriously as an evil sorceress as Celestina undoubtedly is at times
in *La Celestina* (*18, 32, 13, 11*), and those who find the dabbling
in magic either a joke (*40*, 237-50) or harmless from a strictly
moral point of view (*7*, etc; *12*, 370-5; *6*, 195; *4*, 138-43). One
suspects that there is a middle path between these two extremes.
After all, since most commentators have agreed that our play
begins in comic style and then gravitates towards the tragic, why
should not Fabia's arts be seen first as funny and then increasingly

[34]June Hall Martin, *Love's Fools: Aucassin, Troilus, Calisto and the Parody of
the Courtly Lover* (London, Tamesis, 1972), chapter IV.

serious as forces beyond her control begin to determine the outcome?

*   *   *   *

Recapitulation of Chapters 2-6

Having explored the background to *El caballero de Olmedo*, let us see if we have discovered any useful criteria for interpreting the play.

(1) One thing that characterizes all Lope's potential sources is that they are elusive or mysterious.

(2) The well-spring is not as clearly the murder of Juan de Vivero by Miguel Ruiz in 1521 as it is usually said to be. The murder is historical fact. It was a localized affair arising, outwardly, from a trivial squabble. There is no evidence that Lope, or even any other creative writer before him, knew anything about the affair, though the documented legal view that the killing was an outrageously unjust murder of a notably honourable man suggests that there were deep undercurrents that bore this petty feud towards the seventeenth-century fascination with *honor*. There is no known prose account that could have served as a likely source for any of the creative writers: the sixteenth-century manuscripts were inaccessible and the seventeenth-century accounts were printed after 1621, based as much upon the artistic re-creations of the story as upon manuscripts or earlier tradition.

(3) The murder of Vivero by Ruiz in 1521 is usually said to have given rise to a traditional song which ran through the sixteenth century and gave Lope the inspiration for a drama which expresses the soul of Spain. There is no evidence that such a song existed. A song known as *El caballero* was a favourite of professional composers about the middle of the sixteenth century, but it was a refined song with words that have nothing to do with the song in Lope's play apart from the fact that it is written within the literary convention of the amorous "caballero". The song has a ballad-like tune but there is no evidence that it started life as a ballad about the 1521 affair. The song in Lope's play is one which (with variants of the kind usual in lyrics both popular and cultured at the time) was in vogue from c1606 to c1620. The available evidence suggests that we ought to look upon the song

as one with music of refined type professionally composed, and
that it became well known only after 1606. It is not impossible
that the words of the song, as we know them, were written – or
re-created – by Lope de Vega himself. We should, then, envisage
the song "Que de noche le mataron . . ." not so much as a folksong created by and for the people but rather as an artistic re-
creation of a legend for dramatic purposes.

(4) Some kind of song of traditional type, alluding to some kind
of ill feeling between Medina and (presumably) Olmedo, certainly existed before 1550. It provides another scrap of evidence that
behind the "Caballero de Olmedo" story lies a history of rivalry
between Medina and Olmedo.

(5) A traditional, literary topic dealing with the amorous "caballero" persisted through the sixteenth century, tending to intro-
duce a more critical attitude towards him so that by Lope's day
there was in literature a characteristically ambivalent attitude
which Lope's plays in general also reflect.

(6) The most likely immediate source for Lope's *El caballero
de Olmedo* was the anonymous *El caballero de Olmedo o la viuda
por casar* of 1606. Lope may even have had a hand in writing it.

(7) The chronicles of the reign of Juan II of Castile probably
provided Lope with much more important material than has been
supposed. Rodrigo Manrique, with his celebrated reputation for
valour and feats of arms, probably served as a prototype for
Alonso Manrique in the play. Perhaps also (see Appendix) the
tension between Olmedo and Medina and the ominous threat of
the Infante Enrique of Aragon provided the historical background for the play. The murder in the play of one Castilian
nobleman by two other Castilian noblemen gains an added
dimension if we see it set against the killing of Castilian nobles
by Castilian nobles in the Battle of Olmedo fought between
Olmedo and Medina in 1445 (and again in 1467) in history. The
murder of Alonso in Lope's play is presented (see Appendix) as
having taken place in 1440 or 1441 in roughly the same area in
which the 1445 Battle of Olmedo was fought.

(8) *La Celestina* served to add to Lope's drama a tragicomic
mood, a sense of the magical or the mysterious, and perhaps other
aspects about which commentators disagree radically.

(9) The vagaries, absurdities, mysteries, gaps, elusive correlations and wisps of reminiscence in the "Caballero de Olmedo" story can, on the basis of our present inadequate evidence, be explained by one hypothesis: That the story was not a simple tradition based upon one particular case of murder but a complex legend (*q.v. 4*, 147) involving many factors large and small. One important factor, for Lope at least, was the enmity between Olmedo and Medina that grew during the reigns of Juan II and Enrique IV. The legend would then have taken shape as it absorbed particular issues such as the murder of Vivero by Ruiz in 1521, a sixteenth-century re-elaboration of the ballad of the *Quejas de doña Lambra*, a refined sixteenth-century song called *El caballero*, the evolving literary topic of the amorous "caballero", a well-known artistic song of the seventeenth century . . . finally to merge with an important seventeenth-century issue – the real-life preoccupation with the rights and wrongs of *caballerosidad*. The prodigious Lope seems to me to have intuited the legendary force behind the "caballero de Olmedo"; it is this sense of deep, mysterious meaning that gives the play its peculiar fascination.

(10) Our survey of the background from several different angles has led to the conclusion that Lope's audience was – and therefore we should be too – predisposed to look upon don Alonso both as a larger-than-life, uncompromising hero to be admired and as a man with an outmoded, remote attitude to be deplored in practice.

(11) Our survey has also led us to the conclusion that most of Lope's audience would have been preconditioned to tragicomedy in varying degrees of the tragic and the comic but that in this play most of them would expect a tragic outcome to predominate since the death of the hero was the inevitable end to the story.

7 "El caballero de Olmedo" on the seventeenth-century stage

This is, after the authenticity of the text, the most important question of all in interpreting drama, and yet it is the one which has to be answered by most guesswork.

We know that theatrical companies at this time (*c*1620) contained a number of actors (those who were most idolized by the public) who specialized in playing particular rôles: the hero (*primer galán*), the heroine (*primera dama*), the father (*el barba*), the funny servant (*el gracioso*), the rival *galanes* and *damas*, and so on. There was rarely a part for an old woman such as a mother or Fabia here (a curious omission which has yet to be satisfactorily explained). Producers (*autores de comedias*) were well used to producing tragicomedies (plays which broke the Aristotelian rules of drama by containing both the comic and the tragic, both noble and plebeian characters) because tragicomedies were, thanks to Lope more than to any one other person, standard fare; but these *autores de comedias* were not often called upon to produce plays which were predominantly tragic, as our play surely is. The plot they were most accustomed to was one in which young lovers slyly outwitted the father (or some other representative of family honour) in his efforts to arrange a socially honourable marriage. Though the stage-figures were based upon stereotypes there was probably far less rigidity in the better plays, at least, than has been supposed; the emphasis, on the public stage, was on the actors and their art not upon scenery or stage-effects.

What might a company of actors, reading through Lope's script of *El caballero de Olmedo* for the first time about 1620, have made of it? What we know of Lopean plays generally suggests that they would have found food for thought because this play would have seemed unusual in several important ways.

Don Alonso

Undoubtedly, the male lead would have found some standard

characteristics in don Alonso: a lad deeply and desperately in love, bowled over by love-at-sight (lines 11-30); high-born, handsome, dashing and polished ("galán y cortesano", 124); honourable to the degree of being touchy and even arrogant (904); willing to indulge in the usual sly intrigue, with the help of underlings, in order to fool the father and win the girl (acts I and II); a passionate lover able – just (*4*, 127; *27*, 303-4) – to control his carnal desires (1654-7) because he loves honour more and because he has marriage in mind, but who suffers on the rack of love in consequence. For some modern critics (*6*, 191-2; *4*, 127), Alonso savours his suffering to a degree that is exceptional if not perverse, though this view is questionable; should we not see in Alonso, rather, the eloquence of a refined, chivalrous lover and poet of the fifteenth century (*42*, 196)? On the other hand, the *primer galán* could hardly have failed to find in the script an exceptional emphasis upon the hero as a Castilian "caballero" of great repute (821-3, 848-54, 1845, 2497-9), exceptionally honoured, honourable and valorous (851-4, etc.); he even shows a very rare sense of filial duty, strong enough even to override his passion for his beloved (1902-11, 2108-10) – an exemplary trait of the kind moralists were constantly demanding of the secular theatre and which dramatists rarely gave them. (We have already noted the significant fact that Alonso in the 1606 play also has this rare sense of filial duty.) There is also an unusual lack of guile in him; though masters sometimes in Lope's, and often in Moreto's, plays rely upon the know-how of servants, there is an almost abject reliance upon Tello and Fabia by don Alonso (1289, etc.; 1791-1804, etc.). He lacks the quick-witted response and resourcefulness that help to save the day in other plays by Lope (*El secretario de sí mismo, El acero de Madrid, Santiago el verde*, etc.; cf 1169-70 in our play), indeed which Inés deploys in order to save the day here (1170-6, etc., 1255-61). Tello does once (1097) suggest that Alonso has become "discreto", but Tello's words (1096-9) are of course ironical: Alonso, we are to understand, is no more "discreto" (worldly-wise, crafty) than Tello is a poet; (the poetic gloss spoken by Tello, 1104*f*, is of course the work of Alonso, who is a poet). When all due allowance has been made for similar tendencies in other love-lorn lads on the Lopean stage, we may conclude that the *primer galán* would have acted don Alonso as a gallant, valorous, honourable and correct hero to an unusual degree, but also as more helpless than normal when faced with non-heroic situations, with matters closer to reality. (This links Alonso with male victims in other tragedies such as *El mayordomo de la duquesa de Amalfi* or *El duque de Viseo*; see below, p. 51.)

This latter point is important because it concerns the way two crucial scenes would have been (or ought to have been) acted. The first is the scene where Tello introduces Alonso to Fabia for the first time (39-40). Alonso responds at once by extolling her "celestial" virtues (41-9). Calculated flattery? If so, Alonso does not lack Machiavellian "discreción" after all. The seventeenth-century actor probably decided against such an interpretation for two reasons at least. First, because of the idealistic tenor of Alonso's words here (and elsewhere). Second, because the scene is written in *redondillas*. Lope, in his *Arte nuevo de hacer comedias*, suggested that *redondillas* provided an appropriate verse form "para las [cosas] de amor". (It would be surprising if any actor at this time had not read Lope's *Arte nuevo*.) Much scholarly work has still to be done on Lope's versification, though Morley and Bruerton, P. N. Dunn and Diego Marín (see *1*, 61, note, *42*, and *54*) have shown us the way; nevertheless, it seems clear that Lope did apply to his own plays as norms (not as fixed rules) the advice regarding versification he gave in the *Arte nuevo*. There is, then, some justification for using these norms as criteria in trying to interpret his plays. Hence, Alonso should speak here in such a way as to show that his thoughts are primarily of love. He speaks effusively to Fabia merely because she is the means to bring him closer to Inés. He has, as usual, his head in the clouds. The scene is obviously comic precisely because of the ludicrous disparity between what Alonso says of Fabia and what the audience can see she is really like; the scene also has the seeds of tragedy because this same unworldliness of Alonso will prove his undoing. He clearly knows something (44-6) about Fabia's Celestinesque arts; equally clearly he has heard about them from Tello (39); the idea of employing Fabia was therefore probably another scheme hatched by the *gracioso*. But Alonso never uses Fabia as a sorceress, only as a resourceful and crafty go-between (*13*, 237-9; *12*, 373-4; *6*, 195; etc.); and there is nothing in the text, with the possible exception of 202-3, to suggest that he ever intended to win Inés through sorcery even if he had needed to (984-7, etc.). Alonso needed Fabia as he needed Tello to supply what he lacked : worldly wisdom, not magic. The second scene is the crux of the play, that in which the mysterious Labrador sings the song "Que de noche le mataron . . ." and warns Alonso that if he does not turn back, his idea of "nobleza" will turn out to be "muy necio valor" (2410-3) – that discretion, in other words, is the better part of valour. The scene is again written on the basis of *redondillas*. Alonso's words are not of love here : they are principally about "nobleza" as he sees it. Does the Labrador, then, represent love? Or God's Love? Socrate suggests that the Labrador does provide a link between the real and the supernatural, though in a non-theological sense (*4*, 156); others will feel the Christian notion of divine Grace is more relevant. However, the immediate point to see is that Alonso would have been acted as the kind of person who would rather die a noble death than compromise with the reality of his own fears and the base threats of others.

Now, we have already noted in approaching the play from different viewpoints, that the "caballero de Olmedo" legend appears to have stood for qualities of chivalrous nobility which the seventeenth century had come to regard as ambivalent. Our first glance at Lope's text suggests that the seventeenth-century actor would have characterized Alonso in the same light : essentially admirable if he had not been so tragically unworldly. Alonso tries to persuade himself that the fellowship of nobility is such that one nobleman would not bear malice against another (2291-3, 2297-9, etc.). The tragic irony behind this admirable yet pathetic sentiment is perhaps the shadow of the Battle of Olmedo (see Appendix). Alonso stands on almost the very spot where it was fought.

If Alonso cut an unusual figure in some respects, would he then have been acted more as a character (i.e. with peculiar characteristics) than as a type? The idea that seventeenth-century Spanish plays did not concern themselves with character-study is a favoured one at the moment; yet Lope's text suggests that Alonso has another facet which in itself gives him some substance as a character in his own right. He grapples with his own "subconscious" thoughts. I have placed quotation marks round the word because of course it is not only anachronistic but also one that has led to a deal of facile misinterpretation of literature. The student may make up his own mind by answering questions such as the following. Can an idea not exist before the word that defines it? (Some linguistic philosophers have argued that we can only think in words.) Does not the belief in imperfectly apprehended thoughts, as in a dream, operate in Spanish literature of the seventeenth century? Does not Lope himself give us several examples in his plays of a man who comes face to face with a figure who turns out to be a projection of that man's own barely apprehended thoughts (28)? Nor is Alonso lacking in self-awareness. He is, after all, a poet (72, 91, 115-8, 160). He is tormented by dreams yet he does not believe in them (1750-1). He is not really blind to the malice ("envidia") of his rivals, he simply refuses as a nobleman to compromise with it (1883-5, 2198-9, 2261-2). He knows enough of his "inner" thoughts to realize that they betray his own secret fears (2269-70, 2273-5), yet he acts knowing that the brave man is not he who feels no fear but he who overcomes his fear. Then there is his extraordinarily moving final lament:

> ¡Ay de mí! ¿Qué haré en un campo
> tan solo?   (2469-70)

Is not this the kind of lament which only Alonso, only this character, would utter . . .?

Compared to Alonso in the 1606 play (44) our hero is more amiable, more of a passionate and chivalrous lover, more of a poet, more endowed with inner life, more dependent upon his servants, more out of touch with realities. If our hero seems at times not quite so admirable as the other Alonso, that is probably because he has more depth of character. Both plays are concerned to present Alonso as an acclaimed hero.

Very few other heroes on the Lopean stage are presented as better men than our Alonso. He is perhaps slightly less exemplary

than the decorous and self-sacrificing don Juan of *Amar sin saber
a quien*, than the barely credible Prince Fernando of *El mejor
mozo de España*, than the equally admirable but perhaps more
innocent victim in the tragic *El duque de Viseo*. He certainly
lacks the guile presented as estimable in *El castigo del discreto*.
He is, however, strikingly superior morally speaking to the
majority of heroes in other secular works by Lope (as far as my
reading goes). Of obvious significance is his moral superiority
over the incontinent Calixto of *La Celestina*, and the petty, spite-
ful, deceitful, touchy, melodramatic young Fernando of *La
Dorotea*, as well as over other "caballeros" such as those in
Lope's *El caballero de Illescas* or *El caballero del milagro*.

In short, then, Lope's don Alonso is far more admirable a
character than most other Lopean heroes; yet these other heroes
are accorded a happy ending generally, whereas Alonso is killed,
as are some of the few others who equal him in moral goodness.
His only error, following the interpretation we have been led to
by most of our approaches so far, is a lack of worldly wisdom:
an error in the eyes of the world, not – one hopes – in the eyes
of God. Is his death, then, a case of poetic justice? We shall look
more closely at Parker's theories, but for the moment let us consider what might have been the seventeenth-century actor's interpretation of Alonso's own answer (as it were) to our question.

> Valor propio me ha engañado,
> y muerto envidias y celos.   (2467-8)

"Valor propio" here has been interpreted as "amour propre", but
is this not a misinterpretation? "Valor" is used throughout this
play (and many others in the seventeenth century) in the sense
not only of "valour" but also of "honour" or "integrity" (2100,
2567, etc.). His act of bravery in saving the life of Rodrigo is also
an honourable act in that he saves his rival (2014-30). "Valor" is
never used in the sense of "self love"; indeed it is unselfish love
for his parents which sets Alonso on the road to his death (1905-
11, 2108-111). Alonso's words must surely mean "My own valour
– my own sense of honour – has trapped me into falling a victim
of envy and jealousy". And he is surely right. His own goodness
was the cause of his death. "Necio valor" (2413)!

Dona Inés

Inés is closer to the standard type of Lopean heroine than
Alonso is to the usual hero. She is high-born and attractive: she
is "de Medina la flor" (68), as her mother was "la fénix de
Medina" (271) and Alonso is "la flor de Olmedo" (2392, etc.)
Her reputation for coldness towards men may well be the usual
coldness towards father's choice of suitors (219-22, 719-26, 1372-4),
for she falls helplessly in love with Alonso at sight (131-4, 223-6,
etc.); this, too, was usual on the stage, as was the notion that
love-at-sight was true love because it showed the couple were
made for each other by "correspondencia de estrellas" (215-6,
1724-5). At first she seems to be an innocent but love soon teaches
her to tell witty lies and to scheme slyly (1257-60). Some critics
have proposed that this deceitfulness provides part of the justification for the unhappy ending. However, heroines frequently de-
ceived their fathers in this way on the Spanish (and the English,
Italian and French) stage in the seventeenth century and were
nearly always rewarded with happy marriage at the end (*El acero
de Madrid, Santiago el verde, La dama boba,* Tirso's *Marta la
piadosa,* etc.). Something other than lovers' deceitfulness must explain the tragic outcome here. Nor can her parody (1257-60) of
the Neoplatonic notions of *docet amor* and Augustinian illumina-
tion be held against her, for this again was commonplace (cf
Finea in *La dama boba,* for example). After some initial hesitation, she takes the use of Fabia as a go-between almost for granted
(252-7, etc.). There can be no doubt that she feels desperately in
need of Fabia's wiles because her fears that her father will marry
her to the hated Rodrigo are real (867-72, 455-60, 1013-39). But
does she hope to use Fabia's sorcery or just her cunning? Most
recent commentators have felt that neither of the lovers uses or
needs magic (*13,* 237-9; *12,* 373-4; *6,* 195; *4,* 138-43) in order to
secure each other's heart (393-6, 806-7; cf 215-27). This, however,
is not the view taken by Rodrigo in the play, for he not only says
that her heart has been inflamed by sorcery but also shows that
he, at any rate, takes Fabia's infernal art seriously (2314-27).
Furthermore, Leonor says that Inés has been foolish (491-500) and
Inés herself says she has lost honour (806-8); there can be no

doubt that she shows more awareness than Alonso does of Fabia's diabolical "virtues" (277, 304, etc.). Because of Fabia's notoriety, then, Inés is in danger of losing her reputation, her good name. Does all this suggest that the *primera dama* would not have acted the part of Inés as a heroine to be admired (and ultimately pitied)? Since she is in all other respects honourable and virtuous, and since she is certainly not less so than heroines in most other Lopean plays, I am inclined to agree with the majority of modern commentators that she is to be seen essentially as a compelling heroine. Further evidence for this conclusion is provided by contrasting her with the heroine (if that is the word) in the 1606 play. Here, Elvira is a bloodthirsty avenger who murders her lover's murderer in a way which may have been intended to be astonishing but hardly exemplary (*44*). Inés, by contrast, is much closer to what must have been most leading ladies' idea of the proper heroine: sympathetic (287, 1251-2), girlishly curious (338-9), coyly feminine (2574-6).

Fabia

A part for an ageing actress must have seemed a godsend to not a few companies of actors at the time.

Fabia's rôle is in part modelled upon the illicit doings of Celestina herself (*1*, 54-5): she deals in quack medicines for and messages between lovers (185-214, 249-51); she is cunning, resourceful and in league with the devil (393-6); she is notorious for her nefarious trade (253-5). Like her prototype, she is good-humoured (434-7, 792-3), sharp as a needle (62-8) and spurred on by a relish for life (1532-45). But there the similarities end. Fabia is mischievous (93, 127-34, etc.) rather than devilish (393-6); even when she calls upon the devil, as in these four lines, we may well imagine that the actress would have taken the scene as one that was funny if not farcical (cf *40*). We have seen (see above, p. 42) that modern critics disagree fundamentally about the rôle played by Fabia the sorceress. Let us now take a closer look at Lope's text. Only Alonso says categorically "no creo en hechicerías" (984-7) (thereby adding another proof of his moral superiority?). Tello protests "me espanta/ver este amor comenzar/por tantas hechicerías" (954-6); and Rodrigo patronizingly forgives Inés because he thinks "te abrasa/fuego infernal de los hechizos [de Fabia]" 2312-3; cf 2383-5). Fabia shows every sign of believing in her own magical powers, but what clear evidence is there in the play of the "bravo efecto" she claims for her "hechizos y conjuros" (816-8)? As far as the lovers are concerned, conceivably an intensification of the passion Inés already feels for Alonso (391-6, 431-7)? But this is very doubtful. What is not doubtful is the appearance of the Sombra and the Labrador (pp. 165-71). For, while the text says that Alonso merely suspects that Fabia has conjured up the Sombra (2280-7; cf *1*, 53), the Labrador says clearly that "una Fabia" taught him the song (2403-8); both the Sombra and the Labrador have been charged with the task of warning Alonso of the threat to his life. If we add to this the textual evidence that Fabia has throughout given Alonso sound advice and sensible warnings (184, 2284-7, 2383-5, etc.), we seem to have a stage portrait of a procuress who cannot be seen as simply an evil woman but who might even be taken as a paradoxical kind of divine saviour. Seen in this light, Fabia the "witch" becomes a scapegoat falsely accused by people blinded by ill temper and malice (747, 762, 792). However, this is probably not the complete picture. McCrary (*17*, 64-71) has compiled convincing evidence that there was in the sixteenth and seventeenth centuries in Spain a serious "witch preoccupation" (*17*, 70-1). In particular, a witch and procuress called La Margaritona must have been well known as a wicked woman to Madrid audiences about the time Lope wrote our play (*17*, 70-1). Another point to bear in mind is that Lope comes down hard in his plays on characters who use sorcery to seduce a girl, as does Alejandro, for example, in *La vengadora de las mujeres*. But this is another issue which the student can decide for himself by a close reading of the play. Perhaps, as Marín suggests (7), we should recognize that the play as a whole is ambiguous and leave it there. Or perhaps we should see the contradictions, ironies and overtones as ambivalence (or polyvalency?) whereby Lope, like Cervantes in his remarkable portrayal of the witch La Cañizares in *El coloquio de los perros*, points artistically to the apparently anachronistic, "psychological" explanation that magic is all in the mind. (And see *28*.) We have already touched on the modern theory that

Fabia's purpose in the play is to point up the moral errors of the lovers (and see below, p. 67).

Pedro

The standard rôle of the father is easy to describe. He was the Argos of the family's honour, constantly vigilant in the interests of *pundonor* and all the traditional proprieties, anxious to arrange a socially suitable marriage, yet either a fool or made to seem a fool even when he is not presented as self-centred, because he was nearly always defeated by the young lovers in their exciting pursuit of romantic marriage. Pedro follows this general pattern, but even he has some relatively unusual traits. He is gravely dignified (2710-1), and his "valor" receives royal approval (2594-7). Though a vigilant "Cato" (1705), he is kind and thoughtful to his daughter (pp. 118-9) to the exceptional degree of suggesting – when it is too late – that he would not marry her against her wishes (2550-3); (nevertheless, Inés and Alonso had reason to think otherwise). Perhaps Lope made this point, though, because he wanted to deepen the mood of tragic irony (*1*, 47-50) rather than to add another trait to Pedro's character. Even so, there are enough traits to suggest that the *barba* would have projected to the *corral* audience more of a character than a stereotype. Fabia implies as much in the text when she jests about Inés's "condición", for "condición" was a seventeenth-century word which came close to our notion of "nature" or "character"[35]; if, hints Fabia knowingly (cf 295-304), the daughters have inherited their father's nature, she would be surprised if they have not already been in love (304-9).

The father, Rodrigo, in the 1606 play is closer to type. Lope's version is, as with Alonso, Inés and Fabia, simply more human.

Tello

In most respects Tello is a stereotyped *gracioso*, the "figura de donaire" (27): a witty rather than ridiculous servant inviting the audience to laugh with him rather than at him (1687 is a good example). Scared if not positively a coward (a "gallina", taunts

[35]Sage, in *Hacia Calderón*, 37-8.

Fabia, 605-8; cf 964-75); materialistic if not grasping (1918-21); a
boaster or perhaps just a tongue-in-cheek rascal (1869-71): these
are all common enough traits in Lopean *graciosos* from about
1610. On the other hand, there are two aspects of Tello which,
though fairly common in other plays by Lope at this period, the
text seems to highlight, especially since they are insignificant in
Tello's counterpart (Galapagar) in the 1606 play. The first is that
Tello arranges matters for his master, encourages him and even
controls him (1791-804, 1269-96, etc.); not only is he a "figura de
donaire" but also, we might say, a "figura de dominio". Tello
was not (to repeat) the only such *gracioso* to be seen pacing the
boards at about this time (cf *Los ramilletes de Madrid*, *El acero
de Madrid*, *La vengadora de las mujeres*, etc.), and the *corral*
audience were to see many more. (One can imagine the satisfac-
tion of the common man in the audience when he watched common servants mastering masters.) Nor is there any suggestion that
Tello or any other such Lopean *graciosos* were being openly
disloyal, since he and they always acted in the interests of the
master (though, with hindsight, we may wonder if such servants
were not a portent of the rise of common man.) But the text does
seem to suggest that Lope has given Tello an extra dose of *savoir
faire* in order to bring out the lack of commonsense in Alonso.
The second is that Tello moralizes rather more than do other
graciosos up to about this date (1620), though this again is only a
matter of degree. Is Tello then, Lope's mouthpiece for the moral
lesson (if there is one) – a kind of seventeenth-century Greek
chorus? Let us again look more closely at Lope's text. What are
the moralizing points that Tello makes? He warns Fabia that
anyone who expects to get on by using magic will come to a bad
end (621-2). But, as we have seen, it is very doubtful if this is a
fair accusation to be levelled at anyone in the play – Fabia
included. He warns Alonso that he should behave with more
"decorum" (898). This has been taken to mean that Alonso
ought to act more decorously, more correctly from a moral point
of view. (Decorum, taken questionably in this sense, is another
favoured notion in literary criticism at present.) Even if this is
the right view, it is certainly not Tello's here. What else can
Tello mean except this?: "Your comings and goings between

Olmedo and Medina are making Rodrigo and Fernando suspicious (890-5, 929-31, 950-5), so make sure you keep your love-affair secret (890-1) by being more circumspect" (898-9). There is nothing decorous about that; and since he both recommends and engineers schemes whereby the lovers may deceive Pedro, there is not much that is morally correct (in an orthodox sense) about it either. The point that Tello is making is the pragmatic one that we have been led to by various routes time and time again: Alonso is too unworldly for this world. Tello does tell Alonso that he is alarmed to see the love-affair "comenzar/por tantas hechicerías" (954-9), but this, I have suggested, is likely to be his mistake. The burden of Tello's moralizing remarks is the danger threatening Alonso's affair, not the propriety of the affair itself (cf 1754-6). Tello, then, is not a moralist in an orthodox sense at all, but a pragmatist whose rôle draws attention to the unworldly pose of don Alonso.

The only other person who moralizes specifically about the alleged immorality of the lovers is Rodrigo (2306-30), and he is the villain of the piece. His accusation smacks of indulgence in detestable rationalization which we, no doubt, ought to be careful not to copy.

Rodrigo

Villain, yes, but a comparison with the donjuanesque, English Count Federico in the 1606 play will serve to show how much more human a character is Lope's Rodrigo. In many ways he begins as a *galán* like the rival *galán* in countless other Lopean plays. He has in act I, though to a significantly lesser degree, much the same qualities and the same interest in marriage to Inés as has Alonso (1369). The essential difference is that Inés has scorned him for two years past (219-20) yet favours Alonso instantly. Despite the fact that Pedro supports his suit (1177-80, etc.), as do the Condestable and the King at a later stage (2601-12), Rodrigo is destined (2042, etc.) to play the rôle of the rejected suitor who becomes beside himself with melancholy, ire and jealousy (461-90, 1393, 2041, etc.). His reaction then becomes extreme to the point where he becomes different from the usual *segundo galán* rôle. Like Alonso (and *galanes* generally) he

equates love with death, but unlike Alonso he speaks in a mood
of deep, pathetic desperation – a point which students could
profitably pursue further (461-90, etc.). Whereas he – and Fernando – began with a fine reputation as "caballeros de Medina"
(1181-6, 2610, 2649), they are turned into "viles caballeros"
(2716) who carry out a cold-blooded, ignoble murder. Now,
there are, I have suggested, two distinct motives for the murder.
One is jealousy, an indispensable and commonplace characteristic of every *galán* who paced the boards. Jealousy alone was,
therefore, unlikely to explain the exceptional, tragic outcome of
our play. The other is what the text insistently calls "envidia"
(2198, 2287, 2468, 2632, etc.). This envy, I have suggested, has
wider implications: Rodrigo and Fernando of Medina are
envious of the prowess displayed in Medina by Alonso of Olmedo;
the rivalry between the two "caballeros" of Medina and the
"caballero de Olmedo" hints at the political struggle centred
upon the two towns during the period of the play (about 1440)
and which came to a head in the Battle of Olmedo in 1445. Hence
the frequent description of Alonso (and Tello) as a "forastero"
(1830, 1475, etc.).

The manner in which Rodrigo chooses to kill Alonso – an
ambush, six men against one – is cowardly and ignoble (2335-9).
To make his case worse, Rodrigo does not even agree to fight
man to man with a sword (2458-61) but arranges for his accom-
plices to shoot from cover with an arquebus (2337-9, 2461-3). The
use of firearms may possibly look back to the use of "diversas
armas" in the 1521 murder of Vivero by Ruiz (*8*, 247). More
important for the play, though, is the point acutely made by
Socrate (*4*, 131; cf *1*, 37): any fire-arm is anathema to any chivalrous knight, and the ultimate degradation of these Castilian
"caballeros de Medina". But that is not all. Alonso, with his
supposition that he can fight his way out with the sword (697-8;
2446-57), has simply failed to move with the times. The noble
sword was not long in being outmoded by ignoble fire-arms.

Rodrigo's claim, therefore, that by killing Alonso he is carrying
out a kind of poetic justice deserved by Alonso for his alleged
dishonourable and immoral behaviour (2306-19), can hardly be
taken at face value coming from a man who is about to reach the

ultimate degradation of outrageous murder. Would these lines
not have to be acted so that the audience perceived that he was
fooling himself into believing that the evil he was about to do was
a good, that he was about to sin *sub specie boni*? And do we not
have to envisage this Castilian nobleman also not as a stereotype
but as a pathetic, humanly wicked character?

Fernando

Compared with his counterpart, Rodulfo, in the 1606 play,
Rodrigo's friend and slightly unwilling accomplice has been
given by Lope a touch of independence in that he has the
"discreción" lamentably absent in Alonso (1370, etc.).

Leonor

The leading lady's confidante, true to type except for one
relatively unusual quality: she is frank with Inés about Fernando's attempts to suborn her (231-6).

The Producer

We do not know which company of actors gave the first performance of our play, though some have toyed with the credible
notion that the producer (*autor*) might have been the actor-
producer-writer Alonso de Olmedo (*1*, 40, note; and see above,
p. 20).

I have already suggested that Lope's *El caballero de Olmedo* is
a play characterized by a mood of ominous tension built up in-
exorably from the beginning in various ways; and that the third
act provides the culminating point in an extraordinary scene of
mystery linked with Fabia's sorcery, the supernatural, the artful
use of a well-known song, the telescoping of time, the terrifying
materialization of subconscious thoughts . . . The producer had
an unusually difficult play on his hands. Nor was that the only
delicate problem of production. Perhaps more difficult still – as
any producer today well knows – would be the problem of how
to balance the comic against the serious. For the apparent disparity between the comic, even farcical, acts I and II and the
tragic last act must be seen in the end to be a natural, a logical
connection. Menéndez y Pelayo (*5*, 72-3) and others following

him (27, 303; *32*, 692; 7, 2-3) have suggested that the play is a splendid illustration of how Lopean tragicomedy worked, of how intimations of tragedy can artfully be shown to be an integral part of the apparently funny or insignificant matters of everyday life, almost unnoticed until they are seen to gather the overwhelming momentum of catastrophe.

I have already had occasion to locate a number of areas of disagreement among commentators on our play. We are now going
to find more. The reader will – rightly – ask why so many
scholars fail so signally to agree (cf *6*, 177). One answer is probably that neatly analysed by Marín (7): the play is an "ambiguous" (polyvalent, rather?) work of art; it means different things
to different men because it *is* a work of art, and a work of art may
(should?) have different layers of meaning which come to light
only if each reader respectfully uncovers them in his own way.
Another explanation is possible, though this should be taken as
nothing more than a potentially helpful over-simplification. Perhaps critics of Spanish literature are beginning the process of
evaluating the moralistic reaction to Menéndez y Pelayo's nation-
alistic assessment of Lope de Vega (and other aspects of Golden
Age literature). At least some of the radical disagreement about
our play concerns the question of whether moral edification, the
apportioning of guilt and the measuring out of punishment,
rather than an amoral enactment of tragedy, is the right approach.

I shall try to map out the main areas of agreement and disagreement.

So far, every commentator (with the apparent exception of
Fichter – see *26*, 443-4) has accepted the thesis that our play is
based on a traditional song stemming from the murder of Vivero
by Ruiz in 1521. I hope that most of us will now agree that there
is no evidence for this thesis. Perhaps some will even find useful my suggestion that our play is better looked upon as the
culmination of a much broader and more complex process of the
evolution of a legend. While there is, in my opinion, room for a
re-appraisal of the nature and function of the song, I see no need
to question the conclusion, almost unanimous, that this song
("Que de noche le mataron . . .") is crucial to the drama. Montesinos (*27*, 305-8) saw our play as a dramatization of the "drama
comprimido" of the song (cf *1*, 50-4). Socrate has the most

stimulating comments about its function : it looks both back-
wards and forwards in a spine-chilling equation of the past with
the present, precipitating Alonso's debate with himself, whereby
his legendary death (linked with the traditional, the popular [?],
the past) jostles with his present dilemma (linked with prophecy,
magic, the future) (*4*, 152-65). I do not find most of this inappro-
priately fanciful. Anderson Imbert (*21*, 17-18) has taken the usual
interpretation of the song as a traditional one a stage further. He
proposes that Lope's play may be seen as an artistic illustration of
how a traditional song is born. Since a number of critics have
followed this lead (*1*, 54; *7*, 5-6; *25*, 504-5; etc.), we had better
take it up. Insofar as a song is "born" in the play, well and good.
But what we know of the bizarre, often haphazard way popular
material is transmitted does not tally with what happens in our
play. The text (2403-8) makes it clear that the song has been
realized or transmitted by Fabia; are we to suppose, then, that
traditional-type songs were created or fostered by sorceresses or in
some other way by magic? In the 1606 play, the lyric has been
composed by a "passing knight" and set to music by "un criado
músico suyo" – a professionally composed song, then? Lope, too,
suggests that the song is a refined one so far as the music goes
(2370-1), not a traditional one in the sense of one transmitted by
popular, oral tradition. In any case, the evidence that the song
was traditional is, in my submission, false. In short, does not
Anderson Imbert's suggestion need substantiation before it can
be used as a valid interpretation?

We have already seen that there is radical disagreement about
the function – though not about the importance – of magic in our
play (see above, p. 42). Lines 2378-9 have provided another basis
for radical disagreement which we have barely touched upon.
Bataillon (*40*, 245 – contrary to his general interpretation of
Fabia as a harmless parody of *La Celestina*) takes these lines to
imply that Fabia serves as a paradoxical means of expressing the
Voice of God. Socrate (*4*, 146), on the other hand, is not persuaded
that the essence of the supernatural here is theological orthodoxy.
Indeed, the possibility that the song is a divine warning is only
one of the explanations that fly across Alonso's mind; and, what
is more, the burden of his words is a justifiable complaint that if

this is the Voice of God, God has spoken too late "ya que estoy en la ocasión" (2380). Nevertheless, the use of *redondillas* could be taken to imply the Love of God expressed through the song, however remote His presence may seem in the gathering tragedy. The best interpretation is probably a compromise whereby the focus is upon Alonso's mind rather than upon externals; in this way, both Fabia and – ultimately – God may be seen as agents of the whole scene involving the Labrador and the Sombra (pp. 165-71). Casa (*13*) sets out to refute Bataillon's argument that the parody of *La Celestina* is primarily jocular (though we should note that Bataillon also finds Lope's play a tribute to the earlier masterpiece), and makes a number of points regarding the serious use of magic for artistic purposes. His conclusion, however, that *La Celestina* supplies "the premonition of disaster and the connotation of evil" of the kind that is "emotive rather than intellectual" (*13*, 242), is unlikely to satisfy everyone. I have suggested that a compromise is again indicated here : since the play is a tragicomedy, there should be no more difficulty in seeing Fabia's magic as comic gravitating towards the serious than there should be in seeing Inés's trick about becoming a nun turn to reality : *burlas* turn into *veras* (2713-4).

There is a fair measure of agreement about seeing Alonso in act III as a psychological portrayal (*28, 4, 20, 23, 22*), a man who comes face to face with his own subconscious fears. This apparently anachronistic approach seems to me to have been proven a valid one by Montesinos (*28*).

There is much less agreement about the kind of hero and the kind of lover Alonso represents. For Américo Castro and Montesinos (*27*, 23-58), don Alonso is the "gran símbolo de la mejor mentalidad española", the model Castilian tragic hero. His qualities, for Montesinos, are impressive : noble and chivalrous; an idealist fatefully struggling with his carnal passions; lyrical, eloquent and refined; adventurous and valorous; yet a Utopian idealist (*27*, 58) almost perversely savouring the "voluptuosidad dolorosa" (44) of his love. In sum, a singularly admirable hero who yet lives on a Utopian plane and is, therefore, in his way a Don Quixote (38-9) : Alonso is the model Castilian hero who has "soñado perfecciones ideales" and "se cierra a las realidades

cotidianas" (38). This approach is that which seems to me most
fruitful; it has been followed also by Rico (*1*), Socrate (*4*), Perez
(*8*), Marín (*7*), McPheeters (*16*). On the other hand, some critics
have managed to see in our hero little more than an anti-hero
(*24*, *19*, *23*), an empty poseur more interested in his dress than
in true honour, or a man so scared when faced with danger that
he is rendered immobile. The evidence offered for such views is,
as it stands, flimsy and eccentric.

Wardropper (*6*) wonders whether critics of *El caballero de
Olmedo* are about to achieve a "breakthrough", as they have (in
his view) with *Fuenteovejuna* and *Peribáñez* (178-9). He suggests
that this breakthrough is to be achieved by viewing Alonso as a
self-frustrating courtly lover who is not so much in love with our
heroine as "in love with loving", at first, and then "with dying"
(189-192). Wardropper argues his case persuasively. Nevertheless,
Rico (*1*, 47-8) seems to me to have Alonso's "morir/vivir" paradox more in focus : love, even more than life itself, is *of its nature*
a sweet pain, a "vivir desviviéndose". Alonso's images of "dying",
though omens of his coming death, are proof of the intensity of
his passion for Inés; beyond that, commonsense perhaps bids us
go no further. However, other scholars have also seen a self-
defeatist streak in don Alonso, including Montesinos and Socrate.
Montesinos (*27*, 303-4) described it as "cierto carácter de per-
versión"; Socrate (*4*, 127) sees it as chivalrous rather than courtly
– that is, reflecting the character of a "caballero" of the fifteenth
century. Now, the notion that courtly love persisted into seventeenth-century Spanish literature is at present a favoured one but
it has been strongly disputed. There can be no doubt that the
legacy of courtly love shows itself in the vocabulary of *galanes* on
the stage during most of the seventeenth century, as it does in
their favourite lyrics[36]. But what critics of our play seem to mean
by "courtly" love is not simply the refined expression of true love
but a self-frustrating passion which the lover does not intend to
consummate. The question of whether the "true" courtly lover
was ever a purely spiritual lover, or whether he used his spiritual

[36]See for example: Edward M. Wilson and Jack Sage, *Poesías líricas en las
obras dramáticas de Calderón: citas y glosas* (London, Tamesis, 1964), nos. 71,
148, 149, 151, 156; 15, 17, 21, 61, 109, 131, 140.

vocabulary as a cover for carnal desires, need not concern us here, because there can be no doubt that the seventeenth-century *galán* used the vocabulary of courtly love (and Petrarchan traditions, etc.) for the expression of true love now in the sense of love leading to the marriage-bed, of mixed spiritual and carnal desires. The *raison d'être* of the seventeenth-century theatre (and of post-Renascence literature?) is marrying for love. The commonsense reading seems to me indisputably that Alonso too is truly in love and genuinely intent on marriage. The student may make up his own mind by studying the following lines in particular: 1638 ("Yo merecí quererla"), 1639-59, 1642-5; 72-3, 176-8, 839-40, 976-997, 1646-59, 2476-8; 1324-32 (*15*, 343-7; *1*, 44 and 57, notes); 888-9, 1252-7, 1610-21, 2511 ("Por vivir os vengo a ver"). W. F. King finds Alonso's language Neoplatonic rather than courtly (*12*). Dunn (*42*, 196) seems to me nearest the mark: there is a "chivalrous ambience" in the play, a "prevalence in Alonso's speeches of a fifteenth-century troubadouresque style of lyricism pregnant with anguish and intimations of death, which moves magnificently from period decoration to genuine dramatic utterance of great force".

The evidence, then, looked at with commonsense, seems to point to the conclusion that Alonso is a true lover who went about courting his true love with marriage in mind in admirable fashion for a fifteenth-century knight (apart, perhaps, from his employment of Fabia) and in an acceptable if not admirable way for the seventeenth century. If there is a flaw in Alonso's character, it is less likely to be connected with his behaviour as a lover than with his obsessive concern for heroics. Lope looks back at our fifteenth-century knight from the perspective of the seventeenth century, and the main subject of censure for seventeenth-century dramatists was the hero not the lover.

Some critics have seen Alonso as a Christ-figure (*17*, 161-75; *12*, 378; *24*; *20*). McCrary and Alison Turner (*20*, 181) even propose that Alonso's death is a resurrection and therefore not tragic. There is perhaps some justification for seeing Alonso (and other tragic victims such as the Duque de Viseo) as remotely Christ-like. He is singularly admirable, generous, "not of this world", the bearer of a military cross, murdered in the context of the Cruz de Mayo festivities (2648, etc.); and "el caballero de Olmedo" does become Christ Himself in Lope's *autos* (*17*, 161); finally, Alonso is described as a phoenix (2703). However, this is another matter where we should no doubt keep our interpretations within the perspective of commonsense. To take the last point only: Alonso is certainly a phoenix in the sense that he as a legend will go on living after his death (2702-5); need we go further? Inés is also a phoenix (1063-5) because she is reborn in the searing pangs of love as the mythical bird is reborn out of its own ashes; need we go further? Lope de Vega himself was known as *el Fénix de España* : dare we think of him as a Christ-figure or even as Christ-like? I suspect that we should have more success if we thought of Alonso as cast more in the mould of the Pure Fool (such as Parzival or Dostoyevsky's *Idiot*).

There is substantial agreement about the high level of craftsmanship deployed by Lope in this play, but this is so far out of tune with what is usually said about Lope's plays in general that we had better focus on it more carefully (see chapter 9).

For better or worse, the main area of disagreement among modern critics remains the matter of how far the play is morally instructive in an orthodox Christian sense, and how far a tragedy that reaches beyond the perspective of Counter-Reformation Christianity. Parker's arguments in favour of the critical notions of poetic justice, diffused responsibility, causality and primacy of theme in interpreting Golden Age literature, are readily available, persuasively argued and well known (*32*; also *33* in part). The weight of critical opinion now tends to be against Parker's explanation of our play. (Roughly for: *18*, *15*, *17*, *24*, *36*, as well as Aubrun and others. For one reason or another, against: Américo Castro, *27*, *1*, *10*, *4*, *7*, *14*, *6*, *12*, *13*, and others.) The dispute has centred upon the thesis of poetic justice, but here we can profitably clear away some misunderstanding. By "poetic justice", Parker does mean that there is (1) "no suffering without some degree of moral guilt" by the end of a play; he does recognize that a work (2) may show "the innocent victim of another's wrongdoing"; he does not mean (3) that the suffering and the guilt need be commensurate; (4) he does mean that Alonso's death is seen from an artistic point of view to be justified

(*32*, 692-3). We need not, therefore, repeat the arguments of critics who have challenged Parker's views on the grounds that Alonso and Inés are sympathetic figures, or that his "punishment" is greater than his "guilt" deserves, for Parker has made it clear that this is common ground. The main difficulty turns upon how far point 4 can resolve the contradiction between points 1 and 2. The particular difficulty regarding Alonso turns upon the fact that most commentators, and the weightiest of them, do not find Alonso guilty or his death justified in any significant sense at all, poetic or otherwise; and upon the related fact that the final effect of the drama is such as to leave us with a sense of moral outrage, the very opposite of poetic justice. A man who in essence deserved to be acclaimed and rewarded becomes the undeserving victim of foul murder. Some of the questions that remain to be answered seem to me to be the following.

Is Alonso not only a sympathetic character (generally agreed) but also a singularly admirable character?

Is his death brought about by any real *moral* flaw or by the malice of others and/or fate? Does his employment of Fabia degrade him, or rather confirm his integrity in that he *refuses* to stoop to using the sorcery of his go-between? (*12*, 368-9).

Is his association with Fabia, then, such that it "justifies the tragedy" (*32*, 693)? Does Fabia cause his death or seek to prevent it? Did Lope link his play with *La Celestina* in order to point to the breaking of moral laws by lovers (cf *45*), or to make Alonso's death more artistically credible, or to intensify the dramatic mood of ominous fatality?

Does the "underhand" conduct of the lovers "justify" Alonso's death and Inés's frustration? Here most critics have concurred in concluding that their conduct is deceitful and therefore morally reprehensible; yet I doubt if this is a valid conclusion, for it does not tally with Lope's own declared view nor with his general practice in his theatre. One of the basic problems that preoccupied writers from the sixteenth century onwards was the growing belief in the right and responsibility of young people to choose their own partners in a marriage based upon love, in opposition to the received idea that parents were responsible for arranging a marriage based upon more socially convenient factors. Marrying

for love is still the cornerstone of our – yet – monogamous civil-
ization. Consider, for instance, the main point of the words of
most "pop" songs. What the student knows of Spanish drama
may mislead him in this respect, for it so happens that the works
often prescribed do not reflect this general tendency (found, for
example, in Italian *novelle*, Spanish *novelas*, English, Italian and
French comedies of the late sixteenth and seventeenth centuries,
and many plays by Lopean and Calderonian dramatists).[37] Lope
consistently, and on the whole sympathetically, applies throughout his drama the "humanistic" principle summed up in the
proverbial phrase taken from the ballad of the Conde Claros:
"los yerros por amores fácilmente se perdonan" (45). Though
he is far from alone in adopting this "we were all young once"
attitude, he does seem to go farther than most other dramatists in
suggesting that there is a natural and commonsensible reason
why lovers do exactly what Alonso and Inés (and countless other
lovers through the ages) do when they secretly court partners
who turn out to be perfectly acceptable to their parents. In his
revealingly chatty novel, *La* [*más*] *prudente venganza*, Lope
ponders the fact that the ill-starred young lovers Lisardo and
Laura never get round to telling the girl's father, Menandro,
that they are in love and want to marry. Speaking as the author,
Lope comments: "Y tengo por sin duda que si luego pidiera
Lisardo a Laura, Menandro lo hubiera tenido a dicha; pero *el
querer primero cada uno conquistar la voluntad del otro, a lo
menos asegurarse de ella*, dio causa a que la dilación trujese varios
accidentes, como suele en todas las causas, donde se acude con la
ejecución después del maduro acuerdo . . ."[38] It is natural for
lovers to want to woo and win each other in delicious intimacy
before they let their parents know what they have in mind. This
novel is characteristically ambivalent and there is – of course –
room for different interpretations, but these words seem to me to
read as a statement *ex cathedra*. Did not Lope understand the

[37]Such as: Lope, *El villano en su rincón* (Lisarda and Otón), *La dama boba,
El acero de Madrid, Castelvines y Monteses, Santiago el verde, El secretario de sí
mismo;* Tirso de Molina, *Don Gil de las calzas verdes, Marta la piadosa, Por el
sótano y el torno;* most of the more comic plays of Calderón; etc. See also 39.
[38]Ed. Francisco Rico, *Novelas a Marcia Leonarda* (Madrid, 1968), 119.

mating-game better than do those critics who have concluded
that Alonso and Inés are punished for courting each other behind
father's back? If all stage-lovers who deceive their parents deserve
to be punished with the endings suffered by Alonso and Inés, we
should have to re-write all but a handful of plays composed from
the sixteenth century onwards, I suspect. I have not read enough
plays by Lope and his followers to generalize with confidence,
but my impression is that the main purpose of most plays was to
induce the audience to side with the young lovers, as hero and
heroine, in their usually successful efforts to outwit parental
plans for an arranged marriage.[39]

My own answer to this particular question, then, is that Alonso
and Inés should not be construed as morally guilty either because
they fell head-over-heels in love, since this serves to show that
they were true lovers made for each other by "correspondencia
de estrellas" (1725; cf *1*, 10, 215-8); or because they court each
other behind father's back, since there was no other feasible
course of action open to them. The reader should not imagine
that this view will be widely shared; but I take comfort from the
fact that it was, as we have seen, a view perceived if not held by
Lope himself. The reason that Lope makes Pedro readily agree –
too late! – to allow Alonso to marry Inés when he realizes that
"el caballero de Olmedo" is her own choice (2546-84) is, in my
submission, hardly at all that the dramatist intended to show that
the lovers behaved badly (cf 890-9), but that "accidentes" befall in
a tragically ironic way: now that Inés is free to marry Alonso
knowing that he loves her and she him and that they have her
father's approval, she is prevented by events from doing so.

Is the Play a Tragedy?

For many critics this is the most important question of all. One
could hardly do justice to the complex problem of the tragic
essence in this play even if a whole book were devoted to it. So I
shall limit myself to some basic facts, some relevant questions, the

---

[39]Cf: "que es casamiento forzado/y contra la ley de Dios", Lope, *El dómine
Lucas, Biblioteca de Autores Españoles*, XXIV, 54a; "es del padre la obligación,/
para salir de cuidado,/dar a los hijos estado/conforme a su inclinación", Lope,
Amar por burla, Obras, Academia . . . nueva, ed. E. Cotarelo, I, 643-4.

most sensible lines of approach made by critics so far, and a few further lines of thought.

Our play was first published in 1641 as a "tragicomedia" according to its title; we do not know if the word was in Lope's manuscript or whether it was the publisher's. The last line but one of the play reads "fin de la trágica historia"; there is no reason to suppose Lope himself did not write these words. After the final line of the play come the words "Fin de la comedia del caballero de Olmedo"; these words are probably the publisher's, not Lope's, but in any case "comedia" here would be used simply in the sense of "play". Hence, Lope may have looked upon the play as a tragicomedy; we may take it for granted that he called it a "tragic history". There is reason to think, therefore, that Lope began the play with the idea of its being a tragicomedy uppermost, and ended it in a mood of tragedy. Many of us will agree with Trueblood (*10*, 309) that our play has "perennial tragic appeal" and that it was the "tragic force that remained with [Lope] most strongly".

There are relatively few seventeenth-century Spanish tragedies. Most of the reasons that have been proposed for this are disputable. The one that concerns us most directly is that Lope established tragicomedy as the theatrical norm; there can be little argument about this; but there is division of opinion about which of his "tragicomedias" so emphasize the tragic that they are better regarded as tragedies (*31*, 204-9). Morby lists forty-two plays by Lope which are either literal tragedies or predominantly tragic (*31*, 187-9). Those which the student of our play should read or keep in mind are: *El castigo sin venganza*, *El duque de Viseo*, *El mayordomo de la duquesa de Amalfi*; perhaps also *La inocente sangre*, *Adonis y Venus*, *Las almenas de Toro*, *Roma abrasada*.

In turning to tragicomedy as the right kind of play for the public of his day (as most playwrights were to do in most other countries), Lope confirmed his intention to change what most theorists had regarded as unchangeable: the classical theory of drama handed down from Aristotle (in the main). This he did in his *Arte nuevo de hacer comedias* (1609). The *Arte nuevo* is characteristically elusive and ironical, but Lope makes it clear that he has not discarded all the old "Rules". Which of these old "Rules" did he seem to apply in composing our play?

Catharsis, whereby the audience is purged (relieved of emotional tensions) through terror and pity. Most of Lope's predominantly tragic plays lay more emphasis upon pity than upon terror or horror; (he moves away from Senecan tradition in this respect). In our play, we may disagree about the extent to which the lovers are to be pitied, but there cannot be much doubt about the way terror is worked into the third act in a very restrained, though subtle and intense way.

Catastrophe, whereby the plot evolves towards disaster, usually involving death. Most of Lope's tragedies or predominantly tragic plays end in death (*31*, 196). Most of them end not in accidental death but in murder. Most commentators find the murder of Alonso a simple case of murder in that it degrades and indicts the murderers rather than the victim.

Hamartia: some flaw or defect in the character of the tragic victim which in part accounts for and perhaps justifies his downfall. Modern critics are undecided about whether Spanish theorists took the "flaw" as necessarily a moral error or not. The student may judge this issue for himself in respect of Alonso. In general, there can be no doubt that most of Lope's tragic victims are more innocent than are many of his characters in plays which end more happily.

Fatality: a sense of inexorable fate that impels the victims towards catastrophe. In theory, at least, such a notion of fate was unthinkable since "no hay más fortuna que Dios" – since it denied the Christian belief in free will. However, the dramatic notion of fatality need not necessarily outrage Christian orthodoxy, for it was perfectly compatible with the inscrutability of God's purpose: what seems an act of malign fate to man is part of His inscrutable plan. Most commentators have indeed found that fatality is an essential element in Lopean tragedy (*31*; 2; 6; *1*, 50; etc.) and in our play. Rico, for one, has detected a deep sense of irony (*1*, 47-50), in the tragic disparity between what is and what might be (an aspect of what is sometimes called "cosmic irony"). Montesinos perceives a vein of irony in Spanish tragedies generally (*27*, 304-8): a duality between man's sentient and in-

tellectual sides, between his fleshly desires and the scruples of
conscience, ending, unresolved, in an heroic submission by the
tragic victim to his destiny. For Rico and others (*1*, 47; *6*, 188-96)
love itself is tragic fatality. Lope, in the *Arte nuevo* and elsewhere, recognized the classical precept that tragedy was based
upon history; and his tragedies and predominantly tragic plays
are based upon history. By "history" he understood not only
"life" but also – as did Aristotle – existing stories (whether fac-
tually true or not). Now, this means the audience watching one
of his tragic histories would, in the main, know the outcome.
This in turn means that they knew the outcome was inevitable,
that their theatrical experience was one in which the victims
were "fated" to suffer and/or die. The use of history, then, pre-
supposed fatality in a dramatic sense. Lope, as we have seen, in-
tensified this sense of fatality in other ways, such as the use of
omens. All this does not mean that the audience did not also
experience suspense (recommended in the *Arte nuevo* as indispensable). The suspenseful emotion of waiting for Damocles'
sword to fall is very real . . . So, for some in an audience, is the
hope that it might not after all fall. Parker (*32* and elsewhere), on
the other hand, argues that inexorable fatality was not operative
in seventeenth-century Spanish drama, and that Spanish trage-
dians substituted instead a system based upon personal responsibility and retributive justice.

The supernatural : shades from the other world. In his introduction to *El castigo sin venganza*, Lope implied that "sombras"
were an irrelevance in tragedies written in the Spanish style. Yet
he introduces a "Sombra" in this play and in others (*28*). His
main objection to stage representations of the supernatural was
no doubt to the effect that they strained the audience's sense of
what was credible ("verisimilitude"). Does the Sombra (and the
Labrador) strain our sense of verisimilitude in *El caballero de
Olmedo*? Not if, as I suggest, we are to understand that the
scenes are essentially a dramatization of the "ghostly" fears and
promptings in Alonso's mind.

"Clara grandeza y superioridad de estilo" (*1*, 46). There are,
as we have seen, conflicting views about Alonso's eloquence. The
play mixes people of high and low status and so would be

accounted theoretically a tragicomedy on that score alone. Perhaps more important, though, is the fact that in this play as in most Lopean dramas there is a mixture of high and low in a "realistic" way which theorists had not envisaged. Rodrigo and Fernando are "caballeros" whose motives are partly elevated and partly base; Fabia is of low status socially, yet her motives are similarly mixed. Some critics would see a similar mixture in don Alonso.

The word "tragedia" itself appears in Lope's text towards the end of act II (1783). The context is Alonso's account of the killing of the goldfinch by the hawk, a passage which has been the subject of some doubtful interpretation (*17*). There can be no doubt that the killing of the goldfinch is meant as a portent of Alonso's own death, and we shall look at the passage more closely below. For the moment we may note that the text is precise about the reason the goldfinch dies :

> y como eran en los dos
> tan desiguales las armas,
> tiñó de sangre las flores.   (1774-6)

The inequality between the hawk's weapons (its claws and beak) and the goldfinch's is the disparity between Alonso's noble but pathetic sword and the ignoble but powerful arquebus. An unfair fight. And therefore an unjust death?

9 Lope as craftsman

Though Lope is often stigmatized as a facile playwright generally, many individual plays that have been studied closely by critics
have been found to show meticulous craftsmanship. This discrepancy can of course be explained partly because only Lope's
best plays have been closely analyzed; but partly too, I think,
because he was not the kind of artist to write plays which make
it easy for critics to discern neatly definable patterns of the kind
that has seduced recent commentators on Calderón's drama.
Lope's plays seem to "work" if we see them in our mind's eye as
taking place on the boards, but we all find it difficult to say
why they work. Wardropper (6, 179) has suggested that this difficulty can be eased if we look upon Lope's plays rather as if they
were lyric poems; Lope, he argues (6, 177-8), was an "anti-artist"
who wrote not so much with conscious artistry as naturally.
There is, in my view, a good deal to be said for an approach of
this kind, but it raises fresh difficulties of its own. One is that we
should think hard about regarding Lope as an anti-artist if only
because he did not look upon himself as such; he was not anti-art,
he was simply (from force of circumstances, not from choice, he
protested time and time again) anti the stifling rules of art formu-
lated by sixteenth-century theorists. On the contrary, he spent a
lifetime meditating upon and formulating his own artistic
practice[40], not to say living the life of an artist. Another is that
such an approach offers one more temptation to forget that Lope's
plays are plays. If we are resolute about looking for drama in the
theatre before we begin to think about lyricism, we shall, I would
maintain, see that Lope's verse in *El caballero de Olmedo* often
comes to life precisely because it serves dramatic functions. In
other words, he is a dramatic craftsman.

I do not mean by this that the poetry in our play is not attrac-
tively lyrical; the lyrical quality of much of his verse simply

[40]See for example: C. Luis Pérez and F. Sánchez Escribano, *Afirmaciones de
Lope de Vega sobre preceptiva dramática* (Madrid, 1961); *27*, 1-17, etc.

speaks for itself (cf. *1*, 58). But to talk only of the poetic attractiveness of the verse is to indulge in the unreal exercise of trying to divorce form from content, style from meaning. A simple object lesson which might serve our purpose here is the sonnet beginning "La calidad elemental resiste/mi amor . . .". It has been examined as if it were a serious formulation of Platonic love, yet in its context in the play *La dama boba* it is clearly meant by Lope to serve the dramatic function of satirizing those who profess to believe in Platonic love.[41] We need not take this kind of objection too far, if only for the reason that the seventeenth century did not: two passages in *El caballero de Olmedo* were published as separate poems in Lope's lifetime. One is a *quintilla* ("En el valle a Inés . . .", 1104-8), first published in 1578, which Lope borrowed in order to present it in the play as a gloss (a formal re-elaboration) composed by Alonso (*1*, 118, note). The other ("Por la tarde salió Inés . . .", 75 ff.), surely Lope's own composition, was published, very soon after the play had been written, as a separate poem (*1*, 74, note). Even so, in imagery such as that related to the eye and the foot (107-110, 127-130) and to dying (155-8), this separable poem is closely tied to the dramatic development (see below, 85).

A more fruitful approach has been indicated by Dunn (42): Alonso's language helps to define him as a chivalrous knight in a supposedly chivalrous age, a nobleman with Christian virtues, a courtly hero who has mastered the art of poetry as well as the art of combat (503-516, 1103-1162, etc.).

More fruitful still is that initiated by Morley and Bruerton[42] and taken a step further by Marín (54). These scholars have shown that Lope, in the course of his life, went through stages in which he sometimes preferred certain verse-forms, sometimes others. Yet, in his *Arte nuevo de hacer comedias* (lines 305-312), he suggested that particular verse-forms were suited to particular moods or contexts. Marín concludes that he did not always stick to his own guide-lines; indeed, we ought not to expect him to do so because he made it clear that his main purpose in the *Arte*

---

[41]*Obras escogidas,* ed. Sainz, 1106-7.
[42]S. G. Morley and C. Bruerton, *The Chronology of Lope de Vega's Comedias* (New York, 1940).

nuevo was to say how he had managed to write successful plays, not how he or others ought strictly to write plays; he did not make the mistake of banishing the "old" Aristotelian Rules of art in order to replace them with any "new" rules of his own devising – the title, *Arte "nuevo"*, is an ironic joke; Lope, in other words, was an artist aware of the need reluctantly to keep in step with the times. A good deal turns upon how far we can accept Marín's classification of Lope's plays and his interpretations of particular scenes. And since Marín takes only 27 of the hundreds of plays Lope wrote, we may well suspect that if we were to study the versification in a representative number of his plays we should find that he keeps to his guide-lines more closely than Marín found. What matters most for our present purposes is that Lope clearly looked upon verse-forms as capable of contributing definable, if variable, meanings to the dramatic content; the verse-forms are, therefore, capable of providing us with valid clues to the dramatic meaning. So far as *El caballero de Olmedo* goes, we shall see also that Lope followed his *Arte nuevo* suggestions about versification with impressive consistency.

Nearly half the verses in our play are in *redondillas* (*1*, 62-4): groups of four lines usually rhymed ABBA, eight syllables to a line.

> O es venganza o es victoria
> de Amor en mi condición :
> parece que el corazón
> se me abrasa en su memoria.   (723-6)

This is a higher proportion than is found in most of Lope's plays of the period (*54*, 12-21). In the *Arte nuevo de hacer comedias* (lines 311-2), he suggested that *redondillas* were suitable for "cosas de amor"; given their simple, natural form and sweet rhyme, it is easy to see why. Marín, though, found that the *redondillas* in his selection of plays were used increasingly after 1615 for ordinary dialogue as well as for expressing reciprocal love or jealousy (*54*, 12-21). In *El caballero de Olmedo* there can be no doubt that they are used generally for "cosas de amor" – for scenes in moods that are explicitly or implicitly tender and loving. This predominance of *redondillas* serves, then, to characterize the play as a love-story.

Décimas are arranged in ten lines of varying rhyme scheme, eight syllables to a line.

> De los espíritus vivos
> de unos ojos procedió
> este amor, que me encendió
> con fuegos tan excesivos.
> No me miraron altivos,
> antes, con dulce mudanza,
> me dieron tal confianza;
> que, con poca diferencia,
> pensando correspondencia,
> engendra amor esperanza.   (11-20)

According to the *Arte nuevo* (line 307), they are suitable for "quejas de amor", and the longer periods and more closely-knit rhyme scheme would seem to be appropriate for a more intense expression of love; "quejas" in the seventeenth century meant a passionate declaration of love more often than complaints. Marín (54, 37) found that they revealed "un estado de tensión provocada por un obstáculo exterior" more often than "el fervoroso sentimiento de un enamorado feliz". But in *El caballero de Olmedo* Lope has clearly preferred them for moments of love that is more fervently expressed than in *redondillas*.

Romance has no set number of lines; the lines are always in eight syllables and alternate lines are in assonance not full rhyme.

> Don Alonso en una feria
> te vio, labradora Venus,
> haciendo las cejas arco
> y flecha los ojos bellos.
> Disculpa tuvo en seguirte,
> porque dicen los discretos
> que consiste la hermosura
> en ojos y entendimiento.   (827-834)

According to the *Arte nuevo* (line 309), it was suited to "las relaciones", and Marín (54, 27-35) finds that Lope did indeed

prefer it for narrative passages, though in later plays it competes
with the *redondilla* in monologues and dialogues of a more
amorous kind. *El caballero de Olmedo*, however, is again in line
with the *Arte nuevo* : *romance* is often used in passages where the
emphasis is not so much on the love interest as on Lope's plot or
the characters' plotting.

Tercetos (of the kind Lope generally used) are lines of eleven
syllables arranged in groups of three, with rhymes linked ABA
BCB CDC etc.

> Muchas veces había reparado,
> don Fernando, en aqueste caballero,
> del corazón solícito avisado.
>
> El talle, el grave rostro, lo severo,
> celoso me obligaban a miralle.
> Efetos son de amante verdadero,
>
> que en viendo otra persona de buen talle,
> tienen temor que si le ve su dama
> será posible o fuerza codicialle.   (1333-41)

They are for "cosas graves", said Lope in the *Arte nuevo* (line
311), and the measured pace of this Italianate metre with its
calculated rhyme scheme does suggest gravity. Though Marín
(54, 60-63) found few instances of such use in his plays, *tercetos*
are unquestionably used for grave matters on the one occasion
they occur in our play (1333-93).

Octavas reales (or *octava rima*) are lines of eleven syllables
rhyming ABABABCC.

> Hoy tendrán fin mis celos y su vida.
> Finalmente, ¿venís determinado?
> No habrá consejo que su muerte impida,
> después que la palabra me han quebrado.
> Ya se entendió la devoción fingida,
> ya supe que era Tello, su criado,
> quien la enseñaba aquel latín que ha sido
> en cartas de romance traducido.   (2304-11)

Narrative passages "lucen por extremo" in these royal octaves, observes the *Arte nuevo* (line 310). Marín (*54*, 41) found that they were used most often for factual dialogue of different kinds, but *El caballero de Olmedo* again bears out the *Arte nuevo* in that they occur in a passage concerned primarily with plot and plotting, as with *romance* but much more grave in tone.

Quintillas (as used by Lope) are lines of eight syllables rhyming ABABA or AABBA etc.

> Ando, señora, estos días,
> entre tantas asperezas
> de imaginaciones mías,
> consolado en mis tristezas
> y triste en mis alegrías.   (2188-92)

Marín (*54*, 22) found that Lope tended to use them more and more at moments of crisis within his plays; this is borne out by lines 2178-2227 in our play.

The sonnet, suggests the *Arte nuevo* (line 308), "está bien en los que aguardan"; it is suitable, then, for soliloquies (*54*, 50)[43]. The only sonnet here (503-516) is presented as composed by Alonso in a love-letter to Inés, and its effect upon Inés is clearly to give her pause, to make her stop and think of hopes of marriage (520).

The versification of the whole play has been neatly tabulated by Rico (*1*, 62-4); by using his summary, readers can easily judge the effect of each verse-form in the context of the play. Some passages could of course be interpreted in various ways. Here are some suggestions regarding the more important of them.

The scene in which Alonso meets Fabia and arranges for her to act as messenger is in *redondillas* (31-74). Should we conclude, then, that the predominating mood is love – Alonso's love for Inés? If so, then we are led to an important interpretation of Alonso's role: his attitude to Fabia is not that of a morally reprehensible man who has calculated that a witch will be materially useful in winning his girl's love for him but rather

---

[43]P. N. Dunn, "Some Uses of Sonnets in the Plays of Lope de Vega", *Bulletin of Hispanic Studies*, XXXIV (1957), 213-22.

that of a lover who sees, ecstatically, a messenger who will bear
tokens of his love to his beloved.

Alonso's response to the letter from Inés inviting him to meet
her that night is also in *redondillas*; his expectations of a loving
reception are explanation enough (571-622). But the following
lines are concerned with Fabia's scaring Tello into helping to
extract the tooth of a hanged man. Does the continued use of
redondillas imply that the success of Alonso's love-affair is uppermost in Fabia's (or Lope's) mind, rather than any very serious
dabbling in magic?

Redondillas in lines 707 to 786 express a mood of love as regards both Inés (no longer an icy disdainer of men : 723-6) and
Rodrigo (who has come to ask for the hand of Inés : 729-786).
The change to *romance* (787-885) underlines Inés's despair at the
prospect of a loveless, arranged marriage with Rodrigo.

Romance is the verse-form for Alonso's set-piece (75-182) in
which he tells how he first saw Inés. Although his love for her
informs these lines too, nevertheless they are clearly more narrative in type than the effusive and tender *redondillas* that come
before and after.

When Fabia mischievously tells Alonso (533-570) that Inés
received her unlovingly, the verse is in *romance*; but as soon as
she admits that Inés really treated Alonso's messenger lovingly
romance gives way to *redondillas* (571-622).

Perhaps *romance* was chosen by Lope for line 787 to the end of
act I in order to emphasize that Fabia is the schemer ("déjame a
mí tu suceso", 882) who devises plots to restore Inés's flagging
hopes that her love-affair will succeed.

Did Lope choose *décimas* for Alonso's soliloquy as his last
journey back to Olmedo begins (2344-73) in order to underline
his protestation of love ("quejas de amor"?) for his parents ("de
mis padres el amor", 2354)? Did he choose *redondillas* for
Alonso's confrontation with the Sombra and the Labrador
(2378-2416) in order to imply the presence of love here too –
God's Love?

*   *   *   *

As Wardropper has noted (6, 179), Wilson's lead in studying
the imagery (metaphors, similes, etc.) in Lope's plays for their

dramatic meaning has scarcely been followed[44]. Though common sense suggests that we should not try to detect symbolism on any grand scale in Lope's drama, we might do well to temper commonsense with poetic sensitivity along the lines indicated by Lope himself in a fine poem written for Isabel de Urbina :

> No ser, Luscinda, tus bellas
> niñas formalmente estrellas,
> bien puede ser;
> pero que en su claridad
> no tengan cierta deidad,
> no puede ser ...   [45]

Images are, of course, materially untrue, but even trite ones may point to essential truths. Let us, then, glance at the images in *El caballero de Olmedo* to see if they point to Lope's dramatic intentions.

Images connected with night are used throughout in ways that are obvious enough though ambivalent. Night invites loving thoughts and lovers' meetings (630, 1058-9, 1367-8, 1654); but it also induces restless thoughts (1758) about "envidia, viento y sombra" (1360-3), horror and death (557-560, 994-7, 1048 ff., 1906, 2066-72, 2360-3). Daylight – especially dawn – is, at times, an obvious, contrasting image of hope (2361-3, 2066-9). Alonso journeys between Olmedo and Medina at night in both the real and the metaphorical senses (557-560, 2066-72); the metaphorical meaning culminates in the spine-chilling darkness that besets his final journey (2360-2, 2374, 2665-8) – darkness in the end prevails over loving intimacy.

Images of death are more frequent still; they are again ambivalent (or polyvalent, perhaps). There is a deep-rooted tradition behind the idea that dying is an image both of the ecstasy of love and the agony of mortal life. Wardropper touches upon this (6, 192 ff.) in relation to Tristan and Yseult; it embraces also

[44]E. M. Wilson, "Images et structure dans *Peribáñez*", *Bulletin Hispanique*, LI (1949), 125-159; Victor Dixon, "The Symbolism of *Peribáñez*", *Bulletin of Hispanic Studies*, XLIII (1966), 11-24.

[45]José M. Blecua includes the whole poem in his *Floresta de lírica española*, I (2nd ed., Madrid, 1963,) no. 197.

mythology, courtly love, chivalric literature, Petrarchan poetry,
the lyrics of madrigals, mysticism, and much else. By the seventeenth century, words to do with dying pronounced by a lover
were much less prone to express any real kind of agony or death-
wish than fervent passion. For two acts of *El caballero de
Olmedo*, Alonso speaks in the latter sense (155-8, 1084-5, 1107-8);

> y a mí sola Inés me mata,
> no como pena, que es gloria.   (1809-10)

But the master-hand of Lope shows in that these trite images,
meant by Alonso to express ecstatic love, serve ironically as
cumulative omens of Alonso's real death. Similarly with trite
references to death as an image of the lover's disappointment
(1252-4) or of absence and parting (888-9, 1611, 1619-21, 2150-1,
2252-3, 2178, 2535-6);

> ¡Ay, Dios, qué gran desdicha,
> partir el alma y dividir la vida!   (1658-9)

And similarly when Alonso is likened to Adonis (861), Leander
(920) or the goldfinch killed by the hawk (145; see below). An
added subtlety is that Rodrigo begins by longing for real – not
metaphorical – death if his love is not requited (463-470) and ends
by bringing real death not only to himself but also to the rival
who has ensured that his love will not be satisfied (1370, 1377,
2036).

So ominous do conventional images become in this way that
even a mocking reference by Rodrigo to Fabia as a "sombra"
(404) seems to hint at Fabia's connection with the appearance of
Alonso's own shade in act III (2257-84); even the Condestable's
curious reference to Alonso's "good fortune" (2100) is an ironic
comment on Alonso's fateful death.

Lope, then, has woven traditional, even trite images of love
and death into the fabric of his tragedy in order to create a
pattern of impending catastrophe of which the victims remain
only half-aware and the audience become increasingly aware.

The phoenix was a common seventeenth-century image and it
occurs several times in *El caballero de Olmedo*. Fabia speaks of

Inés's mother as "la fénix de Medina" (271). Since there was supposed to be only one such bird in existence at any one given time (a new bird did not arise until born from the dead parent's ashes[46]), "phoenix" became a catchword for "peerless"; this is clearly what Fabia means, in the first place, here. But the basic meaning of the phoenix was rebirth or regeneration[47], and since Fabia's purpose is to extol the beauty of the daughter rather than the mother (as when, in a *piropo*, "¡Viva tu madre!" is aimed at the daughter), this image is implied too: the mother's peerless beauty is regenerated in Inés. Alonso is also spoken of as a phoenix; this occurs after his murder, as Tello declares that his fame will live on (2703-5) – that he will be regenerated. Perhaps the image also implies that the stage figure of Alonso was itself a regeneration of the dead Alonso in history (2270, etc.). Less obvious is the meaning of the imagery of Inés's amorous words to Alonso:

> Como mariposa llego
> a estas horas, deseosa
> de tu luz . . . No mariposa,
> fénix ya, pues de una suerte
> me da vida y me da muerte
> llama tan dulce y hermosa.   (1060-5)

The moth as a metaphor of the lover drawn irresistibly to his death in the flames of passion was one of the most persistent images in European poetry from Petrarch onwards, but the association of the moth ("mariposa") with the phoenix (1062-3) was less common. For elucidation we may turn to a remarkable sonnet by Diego Hurtado de Mendoza:

> Cual simple mariposa vuelvo al fuego
> de vuestra hermosura do me abraso,
> y cuando siento el daño y huyo el paso
> Amor me torna allí por fuerza luego.
> No bastan a aliviarme fuerza o ruego,

[46]See Sage, "The Constant Phoenix. Text and Performance of *El príncipe constante*", *Studia Iberica: Festschrift für Hans Flasche* (Berne, 1973), 569-70, 573-4.

[47]*Ibid.*, 569.

> y si es que alguna vez me escapo acaso,
> hallo que Amor me está aguardando el paso,
> y tórname, cual fugitivo, al fuego.
> Yo, viendo ya que con vivir no puedo
> huir de mi destino y fiera suerte,
> deseoso en tanto mal de algún sosiego,
> perdido a mi tormento todo el miedo,
> buscando como fénix vida en muerte,
> cual simple mariposa vuelvo al fuego.[48]

The fascination of Mendoza's sonnet comes partly from its ambivalence: the lover, in the image of the phoenix, hopes that he will win renewed life if he gives free rein to his passion, and yet, in the image of the moth, he fears that he will be scorched to death; the moth, being equated with the phoenix, goes through the endless, cyclic process of death and rebirth only to be tortured again and again (though there are cunningly optimistic overtones); the form of the poem artfully matches this cyclic process, for the last line is the first. With this splendid prototype in mind, we can see more clearly how Lope's imagery points in a different direction: Inés, in declaring that she is not a moth but a phoenix (1062-3), speaks not pessimistically in the expectation of any real pain or death but within the optimistic tradition of the phoenix whereby death is a metaphorical dying that brings renewed life:

> me da vida y me da muerte
> llama tan dulce y hermosa.   (1063-5)

But, once again, Lope implies the ironical twist that, unknown to Inés, the outcome will be real death for Alonso and virtual death for herself. Similarly, in Alonso's poem recited by Tello (1113-62), the *morir/vivir* conceit surely relates in the first place to Alonso's undying love, but does it not hint also at his real death?

Many other images in the play would repay careful study. For instance: Those centred round reciprocal love ("correspondencias", "estrellas", etc: 1-30, 215-8, 986-7, etc; form and matter:

---

[48]"Oeuvres attribuées", ed. Foulché-Delbosc, *Revue Hispanique*, XXXII (1914), 51.

3-4, and see *42*); melancholy and sadness (in Alonso: 2210-2243, 2273-7, 2347-53, 2373, 2399, etc; in Inés: 2528, etc; in Rodrigo: 1354-6, etc.); dawn (felicitous: 78, 1328-30, etc; or ominous: 1324-7, 1027, 1757-64); enmity and envy (1325, 1715, 2163-5; in relation to Rodrigo in particular: 1361, 2065, 2286-2305; in relation to Rodrigo, Fernando and the nobles of Medina generally: 1883-4, 2007-9, 2198-2200, 2468, 2613); the traditional tribute of "la gala y la flor" (in relation to Inés: 68, etc; to her mother: 280; to Alonso: 885-7, 2391-2, etc.); Inés as *labradora/señora* (64-6, 70-1, 137-8, etc.).

Images of valour are important in establishing Alonso as a knight who equates honour with wielding the sword yet who is killed by an ignoble but ironically more advanced firearm (698, "una Sombra . . . puesta la mano en el puño de la espada" on p. 165, 2266, 2499, 2667, 2338, 2458-63); and finally as a hero whose very bravery is his undoing (2099-2101, 2357, 2412, 2567, 2596).

The image of the cross has been seen as implying that Alonso is a kind of Christ-figure, but here I think we should take care to keep our sense of proportion. We might add, though, a note on the image of the "caballero". Fabia pretends that Inés has decided to take the veil – to espouse Christ "que es muy noble caballero" (1425), though everyone except Pedro knows that her "caballero" is really Alonso. Now, a situation of this kind whereby a joke turns into a fact, a piece of burlesque points to a serious truth, was a standard technique in the Lopean theatre. Lope (*Arte nuevo de hacer comedias*, lines 319-322) calls the technique "engañar con la verdad"; it falls within the sixteenth- and seventeenth-century tradition of "burlas veras"[49]. Hence, when Tello, in recounting the death of Alonso (2647-51), links the Cruz de Mayo festivities specifically with the Passion (2651), we clearly have another instance of "burlas veras" – of a joke that has become only too true. This sense of the ironically comic-serious nature of the world seems to me to be more important to the play than any Christ-like features in Alonso.

Several commentators have noted the emphasis upon eyes and sight in the play; most have concluded that this shows that

[49] Cf J. Fernández Montesinos, *Teatro antiguo español*, IV (Madrid, 1922), 160-3; *39*, 254.

Alonso is a self-preoccupied lover who merely dallies with Inés in
the courtly-love mould (see 6, 185 ff.). I think that a proper study
of these images in the context of the play and their literary background would show that this interpretation is wrong. Briefly:
In Lope's lifetime, the eyes of a girl had already become established in poetic tradition as a source of otherworldly beauty
because the eyes were the windows of the soul[50]. Hence the lover
who extolled a girl's eyes showed that he was unlikely to be just
sensually attracted but was, rather, truly in love. In El caballero
de Olmedo, images of the eyes and of seeing are woven in with
other Petrarchan commonplaces (such as the girl's hair – see 1,
107, note), generally depicting the genuine quality of the love
Alonso and Inés have for each other (12-30, 55-61, 166-170, 237-
240, 2683; 1987; 256, 550-1, 1013-4; 25 and 229). That they were
truly in love does not of course mean that they were not sensually
excited by each other; the eyes, as instruments of sensory percep-
tion, were often held to be more easily seduced by sensual beauty
than the ears (which could apprehend true harmony – the voice
of God[51]; cf. 1, 82, note). There can be no doubt that Alonso sees
and falls in love with Inés's physical beauty; what is most striking
about Lope's technique for implying this is the adroit way he has
associated the image of the eye with the image of the foot, for, if
the girl's eyes evoked spiritual feelings, her foot was (so long as
skirts were ankle-length) an object inciting sensual curiosity:

> Unas doradas chinelas,
> presas de un blanco listón,
> engastaban unos pies
> que fueran manos de amor . . .
> descubriendo medias blancas
> poco espacio, de temor
> de que no pudieran serlo
> sin esta justa atención . . .

[50]Cf note 38, for example. A girl's eyes often gave rise, nevertheless, to a
conceited paradox because they were a source both of light ("estrellas" etc.) and
fire ("fuego" – of passion). See Lope, Rimas, ed. Gerardo Diego (Madrid, 1963),
117, 179, 248, 127, 133, 139, 146, 208, 230, 267, etc.

[51]Sage, "The Function of Music in the Theatre of Calderón", Critical Studies
of Calderón's "Comedias", vol. XIX of Pedro Calderón de la Barca, Comedias,
ed. D. W. Cruickshank and J. E. Varey (London, 1973), 209-30.

que, con esta misma acción,
la bellísima Amarilis
un arroyuelo saltó.
Riéronse los cristales;
¡ojalá tuvieran voz,
porque dijeran su dicha
sin murmurar la ocasión! . . .[52]

Is it not clear that Lope combines these two images of the eye and
the foot consistently in our play in order to show that the love of
Alonso and Inés for each other is a mixture – perfectly legitimate
– of the spiritual and the sensual (107-110, 507-516, 830-8, 1113-
27)?

The image of the play which has received most attention from
critics is that of the goldfinch and the hawk (1763-90; *17*); most
of the interpretations offered seem to me as esoteric as they do to
Rico (*1*, 58, note). As always, we must be careful to build on
what Lope's text in fact says. Alonso recounts (1757-90) that, one
fine morning, he awoke after a restless night and watched a
goldfinch alight upon some green broom where its bright plum-
age mingled with the yellow blooms and the green foliage; while
it was singing of its love, a hawk, lurking in an almond tree,
swooped and, "como eran en los dos/tan desiguales las armas",
killed it; the goldfinch's mate, perched in a jasmine tree, was a
witness to this tragedy; Alonso links what he has seen with
dreams – unspecified but ominous – he has had and, despite his
assertion of disbelief in omens, is dismayed. There is, then, no
doubt that Alonso, despite himself, fears that the killing of the
goldfinch is a premonition of his own death; it seems to follow
that the hawk is a metaphor of Rodrigo the murderer. To meet
the obvious objection that Alonso is not precisely, not "formally"
a goldfinch, nor Inés a widowed bird, nor Rodrigo a hawk in a
variety of senses, we need only turn again to Lope's poem "No
ser, Luscinda, tus bellas/niñas" (see above, 83); there is an essential correlation between the three birds and the three protagonists.
The goldfinch often figured in literature and in emblems of the
period (we should beware of anachronistic notions) as a bird

[52]Lope, *La Dorotea,* ed. J. M. Blecua (Madrid, 1955), 165; cf 196, 198, 250.

that was brightly coloured, joyful and loving yet "ignorante"[53].
Alonso too is a brilliant, attractive hero who is, in my submission
(behind the jargon of the courtly and chivalrous lover), essentially
happy. But is he "ignorante"? This word could carry several
meanings in the seventeenth century[54], from simple innocence to
culpable ignorance; the exact point between these two extremes
upon which we ought to place Alonso is no doubt a matter for
debate, but commonsense seems to suggest that this goldfinch
was, if a trifle rash, essentially innocent, and that the same therefore goes for Alonso. The hawk, obviously the villain of the
piece, was perhaps intended by Lope to pinpoint the ignobility of
Rodrigo's murderous attack; according to at least one seventeenth-
century authority[55], the "azor" was one of the least noble members of the hawk family.

Commonsense also seems to suggest that, since the fight between the hawk and the goldfinch was unfair in view of the disparity between their weapons (claws and beaks, 1775), Alonso's
death was also unjust insofar as the same phrase ("tan desiguales
las armas", 1775) applies even more poignantly to the disparity
between a sword and an arquebus (2458-63). And since Lope has
used the word "tragedia" (1783) of this unjust killing of the goldfinch, are we not bound to conclude that the tragedy in the play
turns partly upon the injustice of the death of Alonso?

We have already noted that there is rare agreement among
critics about the masterly way Lope has merged comedy into
tragedy, and grafted the song onto the drama. We might note
that there is another way which might help to explain Lope's
subtle structuring of his plays: correlations (parallels and con-

[53]"Su amiga Pradelia había puesto en un óvalo, un jilguero en un ramo, asido
a unas varetas de liga, con una letra que decía: 'Mi ignorancia' ", Lope, *La
Arcadia,* ed. Entrambasaguas, 151. One of Covarrubias's emblems represents
the goldfinch as ceasing to be unintelligent when motivated by hunger: Sebastián
de Covarrubias Orozco, *Emblemas morales* (Madrid, 1610), *emblema* 59.
"Confiado jilguerillo . . . " were the first words of a well-known song of
the seventeenth and eighteenth centuries (a version by A. Literes is extant):
here too the bird is pathetically innocent though rash.

[54]See for instance: Sebastián de Covarrubias, *Tesoro de la lengua castellana o
española* [1611], ed. M. de Riquer (Barcelona, 1943), under "ignorancia".

[55]Andrés Ferrer de Valdecebro, *Govierno general, moral, y politico hallado en
las fieras, y animales sylvestres* (Barcelona, 1696), 224.

trasts of various kinds) of the sort that has been more often seen in the theatre of Calderón. As when act I ends with Fabia's encouraging a hesitant Inés, and act II ends with Tello's encouraging a despairing Alonso; or when Inés is presented to Alonso as "de Medina la flor" (68) and Alonso to Inés as "la flor de Olmedo" (887, etc.).

But if there is one moment which for me sums up Lope's elusive craftsmanship, it is Alonso's surprisingly moving words when he realizes that he is in truth about to die –

> ¡Ay de mí! ¿Qué haré en un campo
> tan solo?   (2469-70)

Lope's artistry is here so delicate that one hesitates to try to uncover his meaning. "Campo" : ¿*camposanto*?, ¿*campo de batalla*? "¿Qué haré?" : even in his death throes, does Alonso still think of deeds? "Solo" : without Inés?, without an audience?, without honourable acclaim? At least part of the tragedy of *El caballero de Olmedo* involves the incongruity of an all-too-chivalrous knight; now he makes one last, pathetic, chivalrous gesture before he turns his thoughts towards his Maker. The rest is silence.

Appendix: The historical background

Lope located his play in the time of Juan II of Castile, who reigned from 1406 to 1454. Despite the appearance in the play of the king himself and his favourite, don Alvaro de Luna, and despite a number of allusions to events and situations pertaining to the reign, no critic so far has felt that the historical background need be taken very seriously. As we have seen, Fita took 1521 as the authentic date for the murder and hence filled in the background with information about the Vivero clan during the sixteenth century; Sarrailh found that Lope's historical facts were anachronistic and vague and that they added no more than a few touches of colour to the drama; Menéndez y Pelayo asserted that Lope picked upon this reign for its obsession with witchcraft and superstition but little else; Rico concluded that apart from some well-worn historical clichés, everything in the play was characteristic of Lope's own times. Only Wardropper (6, 182) has gone on record as suggesting that we may not have got to the bottom of Lope's alleged "tampering with history". (Wardropper has in mind here the hypothesis that Lope called our hero and heroine Alonso and Inés because these were the names of the grandparents of the Juan de Vivero who was murdered in 1521; Rico – *1*, 44, note – regards this as mere coincidence.)

That Lope based some of his plays upon various chronicles of Spanish history, available to him in printed editions of the sixteenth century, is beyond dispute. That he sometimes followed a chronicle closely and sometimes (as in *El duque de Viseo*, for instance) carefully diverged from his source, is also beyond dispute.

In the following pages I shall outline the case for concluding that Lope made careful use of a chronicle or of chronicles in this play too, that he placed the action in the reign of Juan II with deliberation, and that we have not fully appreciated the drama until we see it against the backcloth of this reign.

My first concern is simply to try to see the reign as Lope would have seen it through those accounts of the period which we might reasonably suppose he would have read; I do not suppose that my analysis will represent anything like a balanced historical assessment, but that will not matter much providing it helps us to see something of Lope's point of view. The basic sources are two chronicles: *Crónica del rey don Juan el Segundo* by Lorenzo Galíndez de Carvajal (Galíndez); and *Crónica del halconero de Juan Segundo, Pedro Carrillo de Huete,* in part revised by Bishop Barrientos (*Halconero*). Also indispensable is Mariana's *Historia general de España* (Mariana). Less relevant and more imaginative are the comments of Pérez de Guzmán in his *Generaciones y semblanzas* (*Generaciones*) and Fernando del Pulgar in his *Libro de los claros varones de Castilla* (*Varones*). Since Lope was unlikely to have known of them, I shall refer only briefly to the documents on don Alvaro de Luna collected by León de Corral (Corral).[56]

Here, then, is a short list of some of the features of the reign of Juan II of Castile described in these books, insofar as they affect our play.

(1) From about 1420 to 1445, Juan II was faced with constant threats of attack from the Infante Enrique of Aragon and King Juan II of Navarre (Galíndez 380*f*, 552*f*, 570*f*, 625*f*, etc; *Halconero*, 10*f*; Mariana, 304 etc.).

(2) Throughout these 25 years, Juan II of Castile, in the hope of averting civil strife, made frequent yet finally unsuccessful efforts to meet the Infante of Aragon and the King of Navarre (his cousins) and settle their differences (Galíndez 404, 552, 654, 570-4, 610-2, 626, etc; *Halconero*, 359-60, 460, etc.).

(3) Castilian nobles began to align themselves behind either Juan of Castile (and don Alvaro de Luna) or the Infante of Aragon (allied with the King of Navarre). Hence, envy and mistrust was fostered between one Castilian noble and another (Galíndez 380*f*, 416*f*, 466-508, 552-67, 570-632; *Halconero*, 33-4; Corral, 74-5).

(4) The mounting tension was polarized upon the two opposing

[56]See p. 38, note 27; p. 37, note 25. Juan de Mariana, *Historia general de España* [1592-1605] (Madrid, 1794),V. Fernán Pérez de Guzmán, *Generaciones y semblanzas,* ed. R. B. Tate (London, Tamesis, 1965).

centres of Medina del Campo and Olmedo. Throughout the reign, Medina was an important centre for Juan of Castile and the royalists, while Olmedo became the rallying-point for the Infante Enrique of Aragon allied with the King of Navarre and those Castilian nobles who turned to their support (Mariana, XXII, ii; Galíndez, 478, 555, 580-7; *Halconero*, 460*f*, 469-72). (This polarization lasted into the reign of Enrique IV at least. See Enríquez, caps. xlii, xciii-cvii; Palencia, II, caps. i-xi.)

(5) Tension built up to breaking-point in the first Battle of Olmedo, fought on the plains between Olmedo and Medina in 1445 (i.e. near the place where don Alonso in Lope's *El caballero de Olmedo* was murdered). Most accounts (by underlining the limited number of dead on the battlefield and so on) carefully leave room for doubt about the degree of valour shown by some of the less distinguished participants; the satirical account of the battle in the *Coplas de ¡Ay [¡Di] panadera!* alleges ignoble cowardice among most of the illustrious warriors as well. (One wonders why critics did not see the hesitation not as cowardice but as praiseworthy reluctance to enter into a battle with fellow countrymen.) Nevertheless, the Battle of Olmedo was seen as the culminating tragedy of a discordant, tense and ominous reign. Tension built up again until it broke once more in the second Battle of Olmedo in 1467, but this we must pass over for now (Galíndez, 627-9; *Halconero*, 469-72; Mariana, 307; *Generaciones*, 52).

(6) Juan II of Castile is presented as a monarch deeply concerned to act with justice and pathetically anxious to do his best to stop the gathering catastrophe; don Alvaro de Luna as a man who was, after fair trial, found guilty of betraying the king and of murdering Alonso Pérez de Vivero, and yet who may not after all have been guilty. The chronicles do not overtly portray Juan as a weak king manipulated by a self-centred favourite, as later historians were to see them. Soon after his execution in 1453, don Alvaro's fame began to grow; in Lope's lifetime, ballads about him were second in popularity only to those about El Cid. One reason for this seems to be that he (like Peter the Cruel/the Just) became a controversial figure : for some he stood as a lesson in poetic justice for the ambitious while for others he was an inno-

cent victim of political envy (Corral, *passim*; Mariana, xxii, cap.
2, 302*f*; *Romancero de don Alvaro de Luna* [1540-1800], ed. A.
Pérez Gómez [Valencia, 1953], *passim*; *Generaciones*, 44*f*).

(7) The chronicles make only passing reference to magic or sorcery, though Menéndez y Pelayo (5, 81)[57] does supply some addi-
tional documentation to support his contention that sorcery was
prevalent during this reign. They do, however, refer to the
apparently "magical" hold don Alvaro seemed to have over the
king in his private life (Galíndez, 491; Corral, 58-9; *Generaciones*, 52*f*).

*   *   *   *

How many of these features are to be found in Lope's play?
His allusions to the reign of Juan II of Castile have been examined with some care by Menéndez y Pelayo (5), Inez MacDonald
(*18*) and especially Sarrailh (*37*). Their conclusions have been
generally accepted (or just taken for granted). Nevertheless, the
notes that follow will serve to suggest that they were mistaken in
some important respects. The relevant passages are these.

> FABIA   El Rey en Valladolid
> grandes mercedes le ha hecho,
> porque él [Alonso] solo honró las fiestas
> de su real casamiento.   (851-4)

This has been taken to refer to the first marriage of Juan II of
Castile in 1418. Although I would maintain that there are
grounds for taking the passage to refer to the marriage of Prince
Enrique of Castile in Valladolid in 1440, I think that the 1418
date is rather more likely, and that Lope had no particular date
in mind more likely still (see Galíndez, 567; also below, 99.) What
Lope probably did have in mind was an essential point: that the
King had honoured don Alonso because he alone stood out during the celebration of a royal wedding, and that the reason he
stood out was that his bearing was singularly honourable, or perhaps that he was one of the nobles who demonstrated his support

[57]See also: Nicholas G. Round, "Five Magicians, or the Uses of Literacy",
Modern Language Review, LXIV (1969), 793-805.

for the King. We should no doubt bear in mind that these words
are spoken by Fabia for the eager ears of Inés and that therefore
she exaggerates; nevertheless, the stylistic conceits (825, 844, 853
etc.) are persistent enough to show that Lope intended the unique-
ness of Alonso to come across to the audience.

> ALONSO   de Valladolid me escriben
> que el rey don Juan viene a verlas [fiestas];
> que en los montes de Toledo
> le pide que se entretenga
> el Condestable estos días,
> porque en ellos convalezca,
> y de camino, señora,
> que honre esta villa le ruega;
> y así, es razón que le sirva
> la nobleza desta tierra.   (1311-20)

Commentators have followed Sarrailh here in alleging historical
inconsistency in these lines, as well as in lines 2081-2105 and 2516-
8. I have not found any satisfactory basis in the chronicles for the
lines quoted, but they are connected with lines 2081-2105 and
2516-8 which do seem to me to be easily explained by events in
the chronicles (see below). In any case, what matters most about
this passage is the emphasis Lope has placed upon three basic
points: First, that the King is to be associated with Medina as he
was in history. Secondly, that properly all Castilian nobles should
support their King (1319-20), though in history (and by implica-
tion in the background of the play too?) only half of them,
roughly speaking, did so. Thirdly, that the King is following
the advice of his favourite, don Alvaro de Luna. There is no need
to conclude, however, as Sarrailh and others do (cf *1*, 45), that
Lope intended to show the King either here or in other scenes as
a weak monarch manipulated by his scheming favourite. Manuals
on kingship published during Lope's lifetime often insisted that
one of the qualities of the good ruler was an open-minded readi-
ness to take advice; another was the ability to act with discrimina-
tion once he had taken advice. Does not Lope's King come close
to satisfying these requirements? There is nothing specific in the
play (and not much in the chronicles either) that overtly points

to weakness in the King *as a king* (as distinct from his capacity as a man). On the contrary, Juan is presented by Lope (and by the chronicles) as a monarch who strives to act decisively and justly when need be (2627, etc.); Tello accuses Rodrigo and Fernando of the murder, the Condestable points to their guilty behaviour, and the King commands them to be beheaded (2717 etc.); on this note of regal decisiveness Lope brings his "trágica historia" to an end. In other Lopean plays, a king's decision is strongly influenced by the feminine voice of compassion: the Queen in the final scene of *Peribáñez y el Comendador de Ocaña*, for example. In *El caballero*, Tello and the Condestable indicate the evidence, but the decision is the King's own. On the other hand, there can be little doubt that we should see him as reluctant (like Felipe II, III and IV in Lope's lifetime) to pay much attention to the more trifling, everyday affairs of state (1554-9), as Sarrailh has said (37, 340-2); especially since the same King appears in act II of Lope's *El milagro por los celos* as indisputably dilatory. If Lope had one main purpose, though, in writing these lines, it may well have been to extol the much-needed loyalty of one man, don Alonso Manrique.

REY	No me traigáis al partir negocios que despachar.
CONDESTABLE	Contienen sólo firmar; no has de ocuparte en oír.
REY	Decid con mucha presteza.
CONDESTABLE	¿Han de entrar?
REY	Ahora no ... Resolví con él ayer ... (1554-95)

The historical allusions here are probably as Sarrailh has proposed (see *1*, 136-8) except for the identity of the Infante (see below). If my argument (that the Infante is the Infante Enrique de Aragón) is right, then the tone of these lines cannot be the self-congratulatory one supposed by commentators who have followed Sarrailh but rather a discreetly ominous one that highlights the political disaster behind the personal tragedy of the finest nobleman in the drama, don Alonso.

CONDESTABLE   A don Alonso, que llaman
              'el caballero de Olmedo'
              hace Vuestra Alteza aquí
              merced de un hábito.

REY   Es hombre
              de notable fama y nombre.
              En esta villa le vi
              cuando se casó mi hermana.

CONDESTABLE   Pues pienso que determina,
              por servirte, ir a Medina
              a las fiestas de mañana.

REY   Decidle que fama emprenda
              en el arte militar,
              porque yo le pienso honrar
              con la primera encomienda.   (1596-1609)

Here again, the historical allusions are probably as Sarrailh and Rico (*1*, 138, note) propose. The dramatic effect of these lines is to emphasize yet again the fame and honour of our hero (1600, 1604); the point is driven home more firmly by referring to Alonso's loyalty to the Castilian King (1603-4) and by linking him in the King's mind with the notion that honour stems from "el arte militar" (1606-9), a notion which links Alonso in turn with Rodrigo Manrique (see below, point 2) as well as with the prevalent, conservative attitude to honour (see above, 33, point 5).

ALONSO (*Lea*)   Dicen que viene el Rey a Medina y dicen verdad,
              pues habéis de venir vos, que sois rey mío.
                                  (p. 143)

In history, Juan II of Castile was often in Medina del Campo, although in the play his visit is spoken of as a rare honour; but this is surely the kind of discrepancy which falls easily within the bounds of poetic licence. What matters more here in this letter by Inés to Alonso is her "king of my heart" image, so forging another link between the King and the hero as a nobleman loyal and true; the image, that is to say, is not just a stylistic conceit but is dramatically meaningful.

> FABIA   ¡Estremado fanfarrón!
>
> TELLO   Pregúntalo al Rey, verás
> cuál de los dos hizo más;
> que se echaba del balcón
> cada vez que yo pasaba.   (1950-4)

Though this is a joke (we are of course to understand that the King was really admiring the feats of Alonso), may we not see in Tello's boastful words an oblique reference to Juan II's own fascination with feats of arms as recorded by the chronicles (*Halconero*, 9-10, 20 etc.)? If so, we have yet another link between King and hero.

> FERNANDO   Es vulgo, ¿no le conoces?
>
> HOMBRE 1°   Dios te guarde, Dios te guarde.
>
> RODRIGO   ¿Qué más dijeran al Rey?   (1852-4)

The envy felt by Rodrigo and Fernando from Medina for Alonso of Olmedo becomes increasingly ominous as the play develops, as we shall see in connection with the next passage. Here, this envy is contrasted with the acclaim won by Alonso from commoners: like the Duque de Viseo, say, in Lope's play of that title, the noble hero is also a popular hero. Yet again is Alonso's name linked with the King (1854). When these lines are taken with the following, do they not offer a hint that Rodrigo and Fernando, in their sour disapproval of this hero acclaimed on a par with the Castilian King, betray a reluctance to approve of their King too?

> RODRIGO   Fuera desto, un forastero
> luego se lleva los ojos.
>
> FERNANDO   Vos tenéis justos enojos.
> El es galán caballero,
> mas no para escurecer
> los hombres que hay en Medina.
>
> RODRIGO   La patria me desatina;
> mucho parece mujer
> en que lo propio desprecia
> y de lo ajeno se agrada ...   (1830-9)

TELLO   Invictísimo don Juan,
          que del castellano reino,
          a pesar de tanta envidia
          gozas el dichoso imperio . . .   (2629-32)

The specific complaint, that Alonso, a nobleman from Olmedo,
has no right to steal the limelight from the noblemen of Medina,
comes from Fernando. Unlike Rodrigo, he is not blinded by love
for Inés of Medina, so we may allow him a degree of objectivity
here ("justos enojos"). Similarly, perhaps, since Rodrigo's complaint that "la patria" (Medina? Castile also?) is ungrateful to
its subjects finds some support in the fact that Alonso of Olmedo
is favoured by the King's officers in Medina, we may allow him a
touch of reasonableness too. Of course, both Rodrigo and
Fernando are motivated at root by personal spite. Throughout
the play the motives for the murder are given as jealousy and
envy (950-3, 1361, 1883-4, 2007-9, 2065, 2163-5, 2198-2200, 2286-
2305, 2468). Jealousy born of frustrated love – this applies to
Rodrigo. Envy of the success in Medina of a nobleman from
Olmedo – this applies to both Rodrigo and Fernando. However,
this cannot be the sole explanation of the insistent references to
envy, for in line 2631 here Tello speaks of "tanta envidia" in the
context of Castile and the King's problems of government
(sugared with a thin coating of discreet platitude : "dichoso
imperio"!). Lope had in mind, then, something more than
personal spite. Our historical synopsis of the reign of Juan II of
Castile supplies some immediate explanations (see above, pp. 91-
93, points 3, 4 and 6) : Don Alvaro de Luna became a focus of
political discontent; more important still, Alonso de Olmedo and
Rodrigo-Fernando of Medina appear as figures moving within
the context of the historical rivalry between Olmedo and Medina.
In the play, rivalry leads to the murder of a noble from Olmedo
by two nobles from Medina; in history, rivalry led to the
slaughter of nobles from Olmedo by nobles from Medina in the
Battle of Olmedo in 1445. The murder of Alonso takes place
between Olmedo and Medina; so did the battle. The battle took
place in 1445; the murder is presented as occurring some four or
five years before. Thus Sarrailh's proposition that the play is

centred upon the years 1410-20 proves an unlikely explanation of
several passages, particularly the next.

CONDESTABLE	Dije a Medina que aprestas
	para mañana partir . . .
	que me ha pedido, Señor,
	que dos días se detenga
	Vuestra Alteza . . .
REY	. . . . Por vos sea,
	aunque el Infante desea
	— con tanta prisa camina —
	estas vistas de Toledo
	para el día concertado.
CONDESTABLE	Galán y bizarro ha estado
	el caballero de Olmedo.
REY	¡Buenas suertes, condestable!
CONDESTABLE	No sé en él cuál es mayor,
	la ventura o el valor,
	aunque es el valor notable.
REY	Cualquiera cosa hace bien.
CONDESTABLE	Con razón le favorece
	Vuestra Alteza.
REY	El lo merece
	y que vos le honréis también.

(2081-2105)

LEONOR	¿Previene ya su partida?
PEDRO	Sí, Leonor, por el Infante,
	que aguarda al Rey en Toledo.

(2516-8)

Sarrailh (37, 349) and others following his lead took these two
passages, together with lines 1310-20 (see above), to refer to the
Infante Fernando de Antequera, dating them 1411-2 (cf *1*, 136-7,
notes). The "vistas ['interview'] de Toledo" (2094 and 2518)
earned Sarrailh's scorn as "encore une nouvelle fantaisie de Lope"
(37, 350) or as another piece of anachronistic nonsense. Neither
Sarrailh nor Fita (nor, incidentally, Castro) found evidence in the
chronicles for such a meeting between the king and an *infante*.

They were mistaken. The point is important enough to demand
a close scrutiny of both Lope's text and the chronicled accounts
of the meetings that did in fact take place at Toledo. In our play,
the Castilian King is restless, perhaps anxious (1554-5, 1558-9,
2081, 2088-9, possibly 2516-8) to leave for Toledo in order to meet
"el Infante" (1571-3, 2092); the Infante shows a similar sense of
urgency ("con tanta prisa camina", 2093). Sarrailh thought that
this passage showed "respect" for the Infante, and on that
account he discounted the possibility that the Infante of Aragon
and his supporters were involved ("ceux d'Aragon", *37*, 348).
Whether the tone of this passage is one of respect or of disquiet is
a matter which each reader may judge for himself, but there are
at least two considerations he ought to weigh before he does so.
First, regarding Lope's text: Would not the actors have to speak
these lines in such a way as to impart urgency and restlessness,
or anxiety ("aprestas", "desea . . . para el día concertado", "tanta
prisa")? Second, regarding a simple matter of chronicled fact:
Juan II of Castile often sought meetings with his cousin Enrique
the Infante of Aragon (see above, 91, point 2), and, in particular
(*pace* Sarrailh) he met the Infante Enrique at or near Toledo in
1440/1 in yet another attempt to avert the threat of civil strife.
Part of the account given by Galíndez in his *Crónica* reads: "De
cómo Pero López de Ayala *contra expreso mandamiento del Rey
recibió en Toledo al Infante Don Enrique* . . . [The Infante
sends a message to the King of Castile] *'El Rey mi Señor venga
en buena hora;* y como quiera que ahora estoy bien aposentado en
San Lázaro, *Su Alteza me hallará dentro en la ciudad'* . . . Y *el
Rey venía de tan gran priesa a Toledo* . . . luego *a la hora el Rey
se partió para Toledo* . . . y envió delante a Iñigo Ortiz de
Estúñiga, y al Adelantado Perafán de Ribera, y al Relator a hacer
al Infante ciertos requerimientos; el cual, antes que los hiciesen,
los mandó prender y meter en Toledo . . . *el Infante* salió de la
ciudad a caballo, armado de todo arnés con hasta doscientos
hombres de armas, y *púsose en batalla cerca de la ciudad en vista
del Rey* . . ." The King and the Infante, however, manage to
patch things up provisionally once again (Galíndez, 553-72; 578-
83, 609-10; the passage cited is on 570-1; *Halconero*, 359-62). Prior
to his departure for Toledo, Juan was in Medina and Valladolid,

and he returned to Medina afterwards (Galíndez, 553, 567-9, 580).

Can there be much doubt that this is the meeting, or at the very least the kind of meeting, Lope intended to conjure up at this point in the play? The Castilian King's sense of urgency, the Infante's wish to meet him (i.e. expressed in the message as described by Galíndez and implied therefore in lines 2092-5), the fact that by act III (2516-8) the Infante is in Toledo waiting for the King, all fall into place. Lope does not at any time say who the Infante in his drama is: he is simply "el Infante". Why the reticence? In part, I submit, because Lope was aiming to intensify the mood of mystery, of the ominous, of gathering tragedy, by keeping this notoriously disastrous figure of the Infante Enrique of Aragon threateningly in the wings (as it were). In part, because the dramatist had only to glance at these chronicles to see that from about 1420, and insistently from 1438 (the year of the death of the Infante don Pedro of Aragon), the two words "el Infante" were used to mean "el Infante Enrique de Aragón"; since Lope chose to locate his drama in this period, obviously we should expect him to use these two words in the same sense. He could not have failed to see also, even if he had not picked up the idea as one of the historical commonplaces of his day, that the Infante of Aragon was nearly always presented as an ominous incitement to discord and mistrust among Castilian nobles.

There are a few more possible scraps of evidence that Lope read the account of events told by Galíndez or the *Halconero* (or some other account closely related). For instance, the names of Fernando and Rodrigo might have been suggested by the insurgent don Fernando de Roxas and his follower Rodrigo Alonso Rijón, named by Galíndez (580) with reference to this same year (1441). Even Pedro's reward of the "alcaidía de Burgos" (2524 and 2593) might have been suggested by events in 1445/6 (Galíndez, 467; *Halconero*, 466-7; *Varones*, 46-7, 95.) But at the moment these suggestions seem to me best looked upon as idle guesses.

What is far from being guesswork is the connection between don Alonso Manrique of the play and don Rodrigo Manrique de Lara of the historical period covered by the play, a connection only touched upon so far (see above, p. 37). Don Rodrigo Manrique was the head of the Manrique clan from at least the 1440s;

since 1440/1 was, in my submission, the time supposed by Lope for the dénouement of his play, the head of the Manrique family at this point would be a logical choice, rather than, say, his younger brother, the poet Gómez Manrique. The qualities ascribed by fifteenth-century accounts to don Rodrigo Manrique de Lara, Conde de Lara (1406-76), are principally these :

(1) He earned an exceptional reputation as "el más señalado caballero de estos reinos" (*Varones*, 95-6). In the play, don Alonso Manrique is said to be "el mejor/y más noble caballero/que agora tiene Castilla" (821-3; cf 686, 848, 2497-9, etc.)

(2) One of Rodrigo Manrique's two "singulares virtudes" was valour, which he prized to the degree that "no convenía a ninguno durar en su casa si en él fuese conocido punto de cobardía" (*Varones*, 49); he associated valour with "el ejercicio de las armas" (49-50). Alonso Manrique is also distinguished throughout the play by his valour : "Es hombre de gran valor" says Pedro (2567), "Valor propio me ha engañado" says Alonso himself (2467), "Muy necio valor tenéis" says the Labrador (2412), and so on (2336, 2015-9, 2099-2101, etc.). Furthermore, Alonso too thinks of himself as "el que tiene/por lengua, hidalgos, la espada", and of course distinguishes himself in act III through feats of arms (1842-3, 2018-9, etc); the King himself confirms this equation of valour with military arts ("Decidle que fama emprenda/en el arte militar,/porque yo le pienso honrar/con la primera encomienda", 1606-9).

(3) The second of Rodrigo's two "singular virtues" was prudence (*Varones*, 49), yet this did not mean that he thought that discretion was the better part of valour, for –

(4) "volver las espaldas al enemigo era tan ajeno de su ánimo que elegía antes recibir la muerte peleando que salvar la vida huyendo" (49-50). Alonso does in fact meet death rather than turn back ("Volver atrás, ¿cómo puedo?/ . . . ¿qué han de decir si me vuelvo?", 2382 and 2426).

(5) Rodrigo fought in the Battle of Olmedo in 1445 on the side of the Infante Enrique of Aragon; he opposed don Alvaro de Luna (*Varones*, 95). Far from suggesting that don Alonso opposes the King's favourite, Lope clearly sets out to show that our hero is honourable precisely because he supports the rightful King. The

emphasis placed upon his loyalty is such (see above, p. 96) that we may suspect that Lope has here deliberately adapted history to his artistic purposes.

(6) Rodrigo was made Master of the Order of Santiago in the province of Castile (*Varones*, 52). One of the characteristic ironies of the play is that the Knight from Olmedo is murdered before he has been given the knighthood which tradition in Olmedo and in Medina already grants him, and which the King intends to grant him (1608-9, 2618-20; cf *1*, 25, note).

(7) Rodrigo's family included two illustrious poets: his brother Gómez Manrique (1412?-1490?) and his son Jorge Manrique (1440-79). Alonso is also a poet (502-516, 1109-66, etc.). Apart from this, there are no obvious links between Alonso and either Gómez or Jorge.

(8) Rodrigo's tombstone carried the legend: "Aquí yace muerto el hombre que vivo queda su nombre" (*Varones*, 98). A moment's reflection will show that this motto contains two notions that are intrinsic to the play: first, that the hero's name lives on after death like the mythical phoenix (". . . cuyo entierro/será el del fénix, Señor", 2702-5), and second that the past is imaginatively telescoped into the present and the future in that Alonso listens to a song which tells how he *was* killed in the manner that he *is about to be* killed (2374-2466). There is perhaps a closer connection here than that which the *vivir/morir* conceit would have provided.

* * * *

To take final stock after this foray into the fifteenth and sixteenth-century chronicles:

Juan II of Castile is presented by both Lope and the chronicles as a king reluctant to shoulder everyday affairs of state; this was a topic related to problems of government in Lope's day too. Neither Lope nor the chronicle account overtly depicts the Castilian king as a weak monarch manipulated by don Alvaro de Luna in political matters (as distinct from personal affairs); Juan himself takes major decisions and dispenses justice.

The chronicles present Medina and Olmedo as the two poles

upon which were centred respectively the nobles supporting Juan
II of Castile and the nobles supporting the Infante Enrique of
Aragon allied with King Juan II (*sic*) of Navarre. Lope, too,
presents Medina and Olmedo as opposing points in the conflict
between Rodrigo-Fernando of Medina and Alonso of Olmedo,
thereby invoking memories of the tragic conflict between two
factions of Castilian nobles that culminated in the Battle of
Olmedo in 1445. Behind *El caballero de Olmedo* falls the ominous shadow of the Battle of Olmedo.

Though don Alonso Manrique of Olmedo is, in the play,
looked upon by the King as a singularly loyal, honourable and
brave nobleman, acclaimed almost on a par with the King himself, he is regarded by Fernando and Rodrigo of Medina with
bitterness as a "forastero". In character, he has much more in
common with Rodrigo *Manrique* (1406-76), particularly in his
emphasis upon valour and feats of arms, than with his other
namesake of the period, *Alonso* Pérez de Vivero.

There is no suggestion that Alonso Manrique supported the
Infante Enrique of Aragon and opposed don Alvaro de Luna, as
did Rodrigo Manrique in history. Loyalty to the rightful king is
the keynote of the play's hero.

Lope's play, I suggest, focusses in the dénouement not upon
the years 1410-20 as has been proposed (although there are earlier
in the drama marginal references to events of 1411-18) but upon
the years 1440-1 involving the crucial meeting between Juan II of
Castile and the Infante Enrique of Aragon in Toledo. The
references in Lope's text to "el Infante" are, I suggest, to this
Infante Enrique of Aragon, presented by the chronicles as a
major threat to peace in Castile at this period, and not to the
admired Infante Fernando de Antequera, as Sarrailh proposed.

Given these references to the Infante Enrique of Aragon, the
historical background comes to provide an ominous tension
which adds a further dimension to the gathering tragedy on the
stage. The murder of the "Caballero de Olmedo" points omin-
ously to the civil strife that led to the Battle of Olmedo.

Nobles who fought in the Battle of Olmedo did so (at least in
part) in the name of what they took to be valour, honour and
loyalty, though their conflicting allegiances betokened what

history sees as their tragic error. Don Alonso in the play, with his (obsessive?) belief in these same qualities, is also seen as both victim of and agent in his own tragedy.

Lope's *El caballero de Olmedo* is far from being just a stereo-typed picture of a bygone age of noble aspirations and chivalrous love. It re-creates the discord and tensions of the disastrous reign of Juan II of Castile, integrating them allusively and yet care-fully into the pattern of tragedy. At the same time, the dramatist highlights those matters which remain problems of his own day : problems of government, delegation, loyalty, valour, honour, compromise. Are they not questions still relevant in our day too?[58]

[58]This short book has long debts to colleagues who have helped me in various ways, particularly A. D. Deyermond, Rita Hamilton, R. O. Jones, A. A. Parker, N. D. Shergold, J. E. Varey, E. M. Wilson; and not least to students who have helped over the years to keep my interpretations within the bounds of good sense.

Selected critical bibliography

Studies of Lope's El caballero de Olmedo in Particular

1. Lope de Vega, *El caballero de Olmedo*, ed. Francisco Rico (2nd ed., Salamanca, 1970). An excellent edition, with an indispensable introduction and footnotes packed with information and stimulating comments.
2. F. Rico, '*El caballero de Olmedo*: amor, muerte, ironía', *Papeles de Son Armadans*, no. 139 (1967), 38-56. A thoughtful commentary on aspects of tragedy, summarized in part on pp. 47-50 of *1*.
3. F. Rico, a forthcoming study of the variants and versions of the legend of the 'Caballero de Olmedo' which is likely to prove important to the serious student.
4. Mario Socrate, '*El caballero de Olmedo* nella seconda epoca di Lope', *Studi di Letteratura Spagnola* (Rome), [ii] (1965 [1967]), 95-173. An extremely thoughtful and stimulating essay on many aspects of the play, based on sound scholarship.
5. M. Menéndez y Pelayo, *Estudios sobre el teatro de Lope de Vega*, ed. Enrique Sánchez Reyes, V (Santander, 1949), 55-87. This is the same as his *Observaciones preliminares* to the edition of the play in vol. X (Madrid, 1899) of the Real Academia Española's collection of plays by Lope. A major essay in criticism in its day, no longer indispensable since its main points have been incorporated in *1*, *4*, *7*, *27* and many other studies; but still well worth reading.
6. Bruce W. Wardropper, 'The Criticism of the Spanish Comedia: *El Caballero de Olmedo* as Object Lesson', *Philological Quarterly*, LI (1972), 177-96. Recommended for its shrewd summary of many (but not all) of the modern critical views of the play, and for a provocative interpretation of Lope's intentions.
7. Diego Marín, 'La ambigüedad dramática en *El caballero de Olmedo*', *Hispanófila*, no. 24 (1965), 1-11. Recommended for its clarity and common sense.
8. Lope de Vega, *El caballero de Olmedo* (Madrid, 1970), ed. Joseph Perez. A very good edition, with an *Introducción crítica* recommendable for its common sense and a succinct summary of Lope's presumed sources.
9. Joseph Perez, 'La mort du Chevalier d'Olmedo', *Mélanges offerts à Jean Sarrailh* (Paris, 1966), II, 243-51. A study of the sixteenth-century documents about the murder of Vivero by Ruiz in 1521.
10. Alan S. Trueblood, review of *1*, *Modern Language Notes*, LXXV (1970), 308-12. Recommended for its penetrating comments on the tragic and other aspects of the play.
11. A. S. Gérard, 'Baroque Unity and the Dualities of *El caballero de Olmedo*', *Romanic Review*, LVI (1965), 92-106. Recommended, though his premisses about the "baroque" and the principles of Lope's drama will not satisfy everyone.

12. Willard F. King, '*El caballero de Olmedo*: Poetic Justice or Destiny', *Homenaje a William L. Fichter*, ed. A. D. Kossoff and J. Amor y Vázquez (Madrid, 1971), 367-79. Presents a case against *32*.

13. Frank P. Casa, 'The Dramatic Unity of *El caballero de Olmedo*', *Neophilologus*, L (1966), 234-43. Presents a case against *40*, and a case for the importance of Lope's references to *La Celestina*.

14. Lope de Vega, *El caballero de Olmedo*, ed. J. M. Blecua (Zaragoza, 1941, often repr.). Edition with introduction and notes intended for Spanish schoolchildren.

15. E. M. Wilson, 'Ora vete, amor, y vete, / cata que amanece . . . ', *Estudios dedicados a Menéndez Pidal*, V (Madrid, 1954), 336-48. Contains some remarks about the play (343-7) in connection with lines 1324-30.

16. D. W. McPheeters, 'Camus' Translations of Plays by Lope and Calderón', *Symposium*, XII (1958), 52-64. Sensible comments by McPheeters and interesting comments by Camus on the play, 59-61.

17. William C. McCrary, *The Goldfinch and the Hawk: a Study of Lope de Vega's Tragedy* (University of North Carolina Studies in Romance Languages and Literatures, 62, Chapel Hill, 1966). Has some useful information on witchcraft and on other works related to this play, but all the conclusions seem over-subtle, eccentric and rarefied.

18. Lope de Vega, *El caballero de Olmedo*, ed. Inez I. MacDonald (Cambridge, 1934), with an introduction developed further in 'Why Lope?', *Bulletin of Spanish Studies*, XII (1935), 185-97. Notable essays in their day, in part anticipating *32*.

19. Lloyd King, ' "The Darkest Justice of Death" in Lope's *El caballero de Olmedo*', *Forum for Modern Language Studies*, V (1969), 388-94. Presents a case against *32* and makes a number of points, most of which seem ill-supported.

20. Alison Turner, 'The Dramatic Function of Imagery and Symbolism in *Peribáñez* and *El caballero de Olmedo*', *Symposium* XX (1966), 174-85. Touches on a few of the play's images to some purpose.

21. E. Anderson Imbert, 'Lope dramatiza un cantar', *Crítica interna* (Madrid, 1960), 17-18. Carries Montesinos's interpretation of the song in the play to an extreme which some have found valid.

22. Helmy F. Giacoman, 'Eros y Thanatos: una interpretación de *El caballero de Olmedo*', *Hispanófila*, no. 28 (1966), 9-16. The 'interpretation' offered is a Freudian one. The surprising thing is that it does point, in wilful fashion, to some psychological factors in the play which seem valid enough.

23. Everett W. Hesse, 'The Rôle of the Mind in Lope's *El caballero de Olmedo*', *Symposium*, XIX (1965), 58-66. Touches tangentially on the interesting question of how Lope dramatizes the workings of Alonso's mind.

24. Alan Soons, *Ficción y comedia en el siglo de oro* (Madrid, 1967), 65-74. See also *1*, 58, note. Eccentric interpretations which some have found acceptable and others may find stimulating.

25. Donald A. Yates, 'The Poetry of the Fantastic in *El caballero de Olmedo*', *Hispania* (U.S.A.), XLIII (1960), 503-7. Communicates something of the play's mystery, but otherwise mystifying.

26. Leon Livingstone, 'Transposiciones literarias y temporales en *El caballero de Olmedo*', *Homenaje a W. L. Fichter*, ed. Kossoff and Amor (Madrid, 1971), 439-45. Unsubstantiated comments, but notes Fichter's doubts about the traditionality of the song "Que de noche le mataron . . . ".

Studies of the Background to the Play

27. J. F. Montesinos, *Estudios sobre Lope de Vega* (Mexico City, 1951; Salamanca, 1967), Collected essays. Fundamental, though they may not seem appealing at first. The most relevant are the following. 'Algunas observaciones sobre la figura del donaire', 21f (including nobility, love, Alonso as a hero). 'La vida literaria' and 'La vida popular', 299f and 304f (including tragedy). 'Dos reminiscencias de *La Celestina* en comedias de Lope de Vega', 101f (and in other plays). 'La paradoja del *Arte nuevo*', 1f (and on Lope's attitude to art and 'enseñar deleitando').

28. Lope de Vega, *El marqués de las Navas,* ed. J. F. Montesinos, *Teatro antiguo español,* VI (Madrid, 1925), 138-69. A study of ghosts and supernatural happenings in Lope's theatre, indispensable for a proper appraisal of the scenes with the Labrador and the Sombra in this play.

29. *El teatro de Lope de Vega,* ed. J. F. Gatti, (Buenos Aires, 1962). After the *Homenaje a W. L. Fichter* the next best collection of critical essays on Lope de Vega (see *12*).

30. Edward M. Wilson and Duncan Moir, *A Literary History of Spain. The Golden Age: Drama 1492-1700* (London and New York, 1971), 43-85 (on the Lopean theatre). Recommended.

31. E. S. Morby, 'Some Observations on *Tragedia* and *Tragicomedia* in Lope', *Hispanic Review,* XI (1943), 185-209. The best general study of Lopean tragedy, though his view of tragicomedy, and of *El caballero de Olmedo,* is questionable.

32. A. A. Parker, 'The Spanish Drama of the Golden Age: a Method of Analysis and Interpretation', in *The Great Playwrights.* Twenty-five Plays with Commentaries by Critics and Scholars, ed. Eric Bentley (New York, 1970), I, 697-707. A revision of the important and controversial 'The Approach to the Spanish Drama of the Golden Age' (London, 1957).

33. A. A. Parker, 'Los amores y noviazgos clandestinos en el mundo dramático-social de Calderón', in *Segundo Coloquio Anglogermano Hamburgo 1970* (Berlin and New York, 1973), 79-87. Part of the argument developed here is relevant to the lovers' intrigue in *El caballero.*

34. A. Domínguez Ortiz, *La sociedad española en el siglo XVII* (Madrid, 1963), I. The most scholarly survey of seventeenth-century Spanish society, from an historian's point of view.

35. N. D. Shergold, *A History of the Spanish Stage* (Oxford, 1967). The standard work on the staging of plays.

36. N. D. Shergold, 'The Other *Caballero de Olmedo', Studies . . . Wilson* (see *39*), 267-81. On the relationship between the 1606 play and Lope's.

37. Jean Sarrailh, 'L'Histoire dans le *Caballero de Olmedo* de Lope de Vega', *Bulletin Hispanique,* XXXVII (1935), 337-52. The best study of the play's allusions to history, but far from definitive.

38. Sage, 'Early Spanish Ballad Music: Tradition or Metamorphosis?' *Medieval Hispanic Studies presented to Rita Hamilton* (London, Tamesis, 1974).

39. Sage, 'The Context of Comedy. Lope de Vega's *El perro del hortelano* and Related Plays', *Studies in Spanish Literature of the Golden Age presented to Edward M. Wilson,* ed. R. O. Jones (London, Tamesis, 1973), 247-266. Has some notes on honour and social status.

40. Marcel Bataillon, *'La Célestine' selon Fernando de Rojas* (Paris, 1961), 237-50.

41. R. Menéndez Pidal, *De Cervantes y Lope de Vega* (Buenos Aires, 1940): 'Lope de Vega. El arte nuevo y la nueva biografía', 65-134; 'Del honor en el teatro español', 135-60.

42. P. N. Dunn, ' "Materia la mujer, el hombre forma" ': Notes on the Development of a Lopean *Topos', Homenaje a W. L. Fichter,* ed. Kossoff and Amor (Madrid, 1971), 189-99. Recommended for its comments on love and poetic style.

43. Lope de Vega, *Five Plays by Lope de Vega,* translated by Jill Booty, ed. with an introduction by R. D. F. Pring-Mill (New York, 1961). Includes *El caballero de Olmedo* in translation. Pring-Mill's introduction includes a presentation of Parker's arguments (xiv-xix), and an application of some of them to this play (xxx-xxxi).

44. E. Juliá Martínez (ed.), *Comedia de 'El caballero de Olmedo'* (Madrid, 1944). Text of the 1606 anonymous play, with a useful introduction.

45. E. H. Templin, *The Exculpation of 'yerros por amores' in the Spanish 'comedia'* (Berkeley, 1933).

46. A. S. Trueblood, 'Lope's "A mis soledades voy" Reconsidered', *Homenaje a W. L. Fichter,* ed. Kossoff and Amor (Madrid, 1971), 713-24.

47. R. O. Jones, *A Literary History of Spain. The Golden Age: Prose and Poetry* (London and New York, 1971). Recommended for background information and ideas.

48. C. A. Jones, 'Honor in Spanish Golden-Age Drama', *Bulletin of Hispanic Studies,* XXXV (1958), 199-210.

49. J. Rodríguez Puértolas, 'La transposición de la realidad en los autos sacramentales de Lope de Vega', *Bulletin Hispanique,* LXXII (1970), 96-112.

50. Maria Cruz García de Enterría, 'Función de la "letra para cantar" en las comedias de Lope de Vega: comedia engendrada por una canción', *Boletín de la Biblioteca Menéndez y Pelayo,* XLI (1965). Touches on this play on 50-56.

51. Mario N. Pavia, *Drama of the Siglo de Oro. A Study of Magic, Witchcraft, and other Occult Beliefs* (New York, 1959). Has much useful, if haphazard, information. Celestinas (30-46), *El caballero de Olmedo* (43 etc.), literary witches (47-51).

52. Raymond R. McCurdy, 'Lope de Vega y la pretendida inhabilidad española para la tragedia: resumen crítico', *Homenaje a W. L. Fichter,* ed. Kossoff and Amor (Madrid, 1971), 525-35.

53. Francisco Antonio de Monteser, *El cavallero de Olmedo, fiesta burlesca que se representó a su Magestad, año 1651, Biblioteca de autores españoles,* XLIX, 157.

54. Diego Marín, *Uso y función de la versificación dramática en Lope de Vega* (Valencia, 1962).